Criminalization of Women

Criminalization of Women

Abortion, Inequity, and Resistance in Chile

MICHELE EGGERS-BARISON

UNIVERSITY OF ILLINOIS PRESS
Urbana, Chicago, and Springfield

© 2025 by the Board of Trustees
of the University of Illinois
All rights reserved
1 2 3 4 5 C P 5 4 3 2 1
⊗ This book is printed on acid-free paper.

This book will be made open access within three years of
publication thanks to Path to Open, a program developed in
partnership between JSTOR, the American Council of Learned
Societies (ACLS), University of Michigan Press, and The
University of North Carolina Press to bring about equitable
access and impact for the entire scholarly community, including
authors, researchers, libraries, and university presses around the
world. Learn more at https://about.jstor.org/path-to-open/

Library of Congress Cataloging-in-Publication Data
Names: Eggers-Barison, Michele, author.
Title: Criminalization of women : abortion, inequity, and
    resistance in Chile / Michele Eggers-Barison.
Description: Urbana : University of Illinois Press, [2025] |
    Includes bibliographical references and index.
Identifiers: LCCN 2025005541 (print) | LCCN 2025005542 (ebook)
    | ISBN 9780252046728 (cloth) | ISBN 9780252088827
    (paperback) | ISBN 9780252048241 (ebook)
Subjects: LCSH: Women—Chile—Social conditions. |
    Reproductive rights—Chile. | Abortion—Chile.
Classification: LCC HQ1547 .E34 2025 (print) | LCC HQ1547
    (ebook) | DDC 364.1/850983—dc23/eng/20250210
LC record available at https://lccn.loc.gov/2025005541
LC ebook record available at https://lccn.loc.gov/2025005542

This book is dedicated to the women who shared their abortion and reproductive health experiences with me. Without your openness to share memories of anger, sadness, and fear and stories of strength and resistance, we would be left without your wisdom to guide us toward creating just reproductive health policies.

And to my maternal great-grandmother, whose bodily existence is a map to mine. Although her original identity is lost, she is not forgotten; to my mother, who in the short nine years of knowing me, managed to instill in me an understanding of and commitment to the struggle for equity and justice. I love and miss you and I am forever grateful; and to my daughter, Melissa, may you always feel the strength of the women who came before you.

Contents

Preface   ix

Acknowledgments   xi

Introduction: Criminalization of Women for Abortion   1

1   Inequity: A Social Construction   19

2   Unpacking Inequity   37

3   Centering Women   59

4   ¡Resistencia!   79

Conclusion: Revelations from Chile   95

Notes   105

References   107

Index   115

Preface

This work emerged from a short experimental documentary film that I produced and directed, *I Choose Me*. The film was inspired by two converging phenomena of the time. First, in 2006 Governor Rounds of South Dakota signed into effect a law making performing all abortions a felony, except to save a woman's life (Davey, 2006). This law was the first of its kind since before the 1973 *Roe v. Wade* Supreme Court decision to legalize abortion. The second phenomenon was the impact of the War on Drugs and mandatory minimum sentencing on the high rates of women incarcerated in the Global North, making women the fastest-growing incarcerated population (Sudbury, 2005). Between 1980 and 2010 the number of women incarcerated in the United States increased by 680 percent (Sentencing Project, n.d.). In England there was a 173 percent increase of incarcerated women in the decade proceeding 2002 (Sudbury, 2005). And in Australia, the population of incarcerated women doubled. Before the *Roe v. Wade* decision, women were not likely to be incarcerated for terminating a pregnancy. However, with incarcerated women on the rise within a culture of criminalization, coupled with restrictive reproductive health policies, I feared the same "racialized and classed" bodies that have been historically marginalized would become the primary targets of public surveillance and criminalization for terminating a pregnancy (Sudbury, 2005, p. xv).

Globally, many countries have gradually adopted more liberal reproductive health policies, particularly concerning abortion. This shift is largely driven by concerns over high maternal mortality rates and a growing recognition of the need for safe and accessible reproductive health services. In contrast, countries in Central America and the United States have increasingly imposed more restrictions on women's reproductive health and rights. These policies limit access to abortion, put women's health and lives at risk, and create significant barriers to women's autonomy, violating the human right to reproductive health and well-being. Thus, the issue of reproductive health, rights, and justice, particularly regarding abortion, remains as relevant and contentious as it has within varying political climates in country-specific contexts throughout history.

While this study specifically examines the experiences of diverse women in Chile, the goal of this work is to shed light on the inequitable conditions in which reproductive lives are embedded, emphasizing the challenges pregnant people face in navigating the complexities of shifting political landscapes. This work provides a foundation for unpacking the complexities of inequity, offering a deeper understanding of how restrictive reproductive health policies construct criminals, while disproportionately harming already marginalized individuals and communities. By examining the intersection of political, social, and economic factors, this research lays the groundwork for a broader analysis of reproductive health inequities. This framework can aid in understanding a more comprehensive exploration of how restrictive policies shape the lived experiences of pregnant people globally.

Ten years have passed since these narratives were gathered in Chile, during which significant changes have occurred, such as moving from a complete abortion ban to permitting abortion under three specific circumstances. Yet, the aim of this book is not to confine itself to a particular period, but to critically explore, name, and ideally dismantle restrictive reproductive health policies shaped by broader systems of inequity. By centering the experiences of those at risk of being criminalized for abortion, the book underscores how these policies constitute state-sanctioned violence and consequent human rights violations. While many actors contribute to perpetuating or resisting restrictive reproductive health policies, this book draws its framing from the powerful stories of those who generously shared their lives.

Acknowledgments

First and foremost, I extend my heartfelt gratitude to the people and communities I crossed paths with during my time in Chile. You welcomed me into your lives, shared your stories, and opened my eyes to profound experiences of pain and resilience. Thank you for recounting the struggles of torture and loss; the enduring impacts of racism, classism, and sexism; and the related effects of living in poverty and violence within your communities. I am inspired by your courage, strength, activism, and organizing for justice in the face of state-sanctioned violence and repression.

I am deeply indebted to the many activists, organizers, feminists, filmmakers, professionals, and academics who shared their work, insights, and perspectives with me during this journey. Your tireless advocacy for women's rights and your dedication to advancing social, economic, and reproductive justice are not only inspiring but also have directly influenced the course and depth of this work. A special thank you to Verónica Matus for your kind and insightful counsel and valuable feedback throughout the years. I am also profoundly grateful to Lidia Casas, whose constant support has been instrumental in the development and implementation of this work. I would also like to express my gratitude to the University of Diego Portales, Center for Human Rights, for your generous support of the visiting scholar position during the eleven months of fieldwork in Chile. I am grateful for the opportunity to be part of your academic community.

xii • *Acknowledgments*

This work has benefited greatly from the intellectual, emotional, and creative support of many friends, colleagues, and mentors in North, Central, and South America: I am especially grateful for the ongoing support of Pam Brown, who has been my inspiration and mentor throughout the years. Thank you for being there through every stage of this journey, for helping me process ideas and normalize the challenges, for offering a space to write, and for your constant love and belief in me; Jud Vogel and Tasia Smith for the many walks in the wild and for your love, friendship, and support over the years; Walter Ernesto Gomez Magallon and Marcelo Villagran Urra for sharing your home and your lives with me; much gratitude to Sue Steiner and Jennifer Ninnis for your friendship and insightful feedback on previous drafts and use of artwork, respectively; Tina Chiarelli-Helminiak, Elizabeth Allen, Rose Murphy, Molly Calhoun, Dilia Loe, Serenity Bowan, Ken Nakamura, Paula Santana, Sarah Cantril, Lisa Fragala, Luisa Garza, and Kenna Murray for checking in, showing up, and holding space over the years in all the unique and meaningful ways you have. Crystal M. Hayes for your solidarity in the struggle for reproductive justice, as I am continually inspired by you and your work; Grahame Russell for the many conversations on the intersections of global harms, human rights, and local resistance efforts. Many thanks to Morella Wojton Mora, Teresa Serano, and Claudia Riumalló for critical language support in the context of lived experience within the broader constructs of inequity; to Margo Okazawa-Rey, Barbara Sutton, and Bandana Purkayastha for your inspiration of gender-specific frameworks that have aided this work to advance a deeper understanding of contexts of inequity and body politics; Megan Berthold, for your thoughtful questions that kept me grounded and reminded me to stay connected to the heart of this work; Nancy Naples for your insightful guidance and for encouraging me to explore resistance in new ways; Kathryn Libal for your unwavering support over the years. Your insights and guidance allowed this work to unfold organically in centering and amplifying women's voices on injustice. You and so many others have been essential to my survival during this project and instrumental in bringing this work to life. I am very grateful.

I am forever grateful to my siblings—Maria, Carol, Randy, and Denise—my brother-in-law, Mark, and my nieces and nephews—Kyle, Blair, Ashley, Sarah, Bruce, Alexandra, Shaun, and Nathan—for your love and for the role each of you has played in my life. To my daughter Melissa and her husband Ben, y mis nietos Rylee and Dylan, I am grateful to share life's journey with you. Thank you to my Chilean family for your love and support while in Chile and for helping me understand the complex realities during and after the dictatorship. Your love and support while in Chile enriched my experience in countless ways. To my parents, who immigrated from Chile to the United States, this work is a testament to their journey and profound love.

Last, thank you to the National Association of Women's Studies and the University of Illinois Press for recognizing the importance of this work with the First Book Prize award. I extend my gratitude to the team at the University of Illinois Press for their support and guidance throughout every aspect of publishing this work. Many thanks to Allison Torres Burtka for your patience and thoughtful editing suggestions.

¡Mil gracias a todos!

Introduction
Criminalization of Women for Abortion

> Where the criminal law is used as a tool by the State to regulate the conduct and decision-making of individuals in the context of the right to sexual and reproductive health the State coercively substitutes its will for that of the individual.
>
> —UN Special Rapporteur on the Right to Health

Chilean Context

I arrived in Santiago, Chile, early in the morning on September 8, 2013, the same day as a March for the Disappeared, commemorating the 40th anniversary of the CIA-backed coup d'état on September 11, 1973. During the seventeen-year dictatorship of General Augusto Pinochet, tens of thousands of people were exiled, tortured, imprisoned, murdered, or disappeared. I joined thousands of people walking in the streets of downtown Santiago. During the march, people were playing guitars and singing; some were wearing traditional Indigenous clothing or costumes, or were dressed as mimes; others were drumming in marching bands or performing traditional and Indigenous dances of Chile; while others held flags and banners representing the Mapuche, Aymara, the state of Chile, Che Guevara, political parties, feminist organizations, and university and student groups, among others; many people were holding or wearing pictures of family members and others who were victims of the state-perpetrated violence; children and youth held signs saying *nada ni nadie esta olvidado* (nothing and no one is forgotten) and *40 Años de Luchas y Resistencia* (40 years of struggle and resistance); while others plastered posters on the sides of buildings with political messages such as *la memoria está viva anda luchando* (the memory is alive and fighting) and *capitalismo y patriarcado avalados del estado* (capitalism and patriarchy endorsed by

2 • *Introduction*

the state) as we marched through the streets. The march ended at a memorial site of the disappeared and deceased in the *Cementerio General*, one of the largest cemeteries in Latin America, extending over 200 acres, where an estimated 2 million people are buried. At the memorial site, people gathered in diverse spaces of music and dance. Although thousands of people participated in the march, while sitting at an altar in the General Cemetery at the end of the march for the disappeared, it was silent. No one spoke even though there were sounds all around. The profundity of the historic and systemic impact of state violence on a people was palpable. *Todo Mi Amor Esta Aqui Y Se Ha Quedado Pegado A Las Rocas Al Mar A Las Montañas* (All My Love Is Here And Has Stuck To The Rocks To The Sea To The Mountains) is written at the top of a towering wall with plaques of people who had died or disappeared during the dictatorship. Most of the plaques included names and ages—24, 17, 18, 20, 21, 26, 16—indicating that most of those targeted were young. It was profound and humbling to witness how people have embodied a memory of violence, loss, and sadness with parallel love, strength, power, and resistance as they navigate healing in a country that still bears the remnants of the violence during the dictatorship.

Participating in the March for the Disappeared upon my arrival in Chile was a necessary beginning to understand the impact on women who are criminalized for abortion within a broader context of historic and contemporary systems of violence and inequity in Chile. Abortion laws and practices in Chile have shifted depending on international and local ideologies and political climates, all of which have shaped women's reproductive health experiences. Pre-1973 coup d' état, Chile had one of the most progressive reproductive health programs in the Americas. In part this was prompted by two phenomena at the time: high rates of maternal mortality from unsafe abortion and U.S. foreign aid to decrease poverty. In the 1960s under President Frei, Chile became one of the first countries in the region to implement a state-subsidized family planning program. Through developing comprehensive reproductive health policies, contraception was made widely available in public health clinics and hospitals. Between 1970 and 1973 under President Allende, the family planning program began to incorporate sexual education and public health outreach. Due to the government-backed support for reproductive health, abortion and maternal mortality rates from abortion significantly declined.

After the military coup in 1973, education and health were hit the hardest due to the privatization of social services and consequent public funding cuts, limiting access to women's health and reproductive health. Restrictive population control strategies were developed and administered under military rule as a measure to protect national security. Under Pinochet's pronatalist policies, reproductive health services were removed from public health clinics and hospitals, and public health workers became mandated reporters for women who suffered from abortion complications. Women from lower-income backgrounds were most impacted. With limited resources, these women relied on public health facilities when faced with abortion complications. Consequently, they were the women most at risk of being criminalized for abortion with the changing restrictive laws and practices during the dictatorship.

In 1931, Chile had legalized therapeutic abortion in cases to save a woman's life. Any complications from abortion were framed as a health issue. However, in 1989, after seventeen years of military rule, Pinochet changed this law criminalizing abortion in all circumstances (Casas-Becerra, 1997; Rayas, 1998; Vargas, 2008). Until 2017, abortion laws in Chile remained among the most restrictive in the world. Much of this was due to the influence of the Catholic Church, which had been intricately linked with conservative politicians, thus a powerful force in regulating political and gender norms in Chile since the colonial dominance of the Spanish.

Choosing Chile as a site to understand the impact of restrictive abortion policies on women had personal, theoretical, and practical applications. I am the daughter of immigrant parents from Chile who migrated to the United States in search of economic opportunities that would not have been afforded in Chile due to inequitable historic and systemic class structures. In 2006, during an interview with Dr. Rebecca Gomperts, the founder of Women on Waves[1] in the Netherlands, on global trends of incarcerating women for terminating a pregnancy, I learned that Chile had a history of imprisoning women for abortion. I was familiar with Chile's history of political and civil human rights violations during the seventeen-year dictatorship after the coup in 1973 and committed to understanding how consequent social, economic, and political structures produced and sustained punitive reproductive policies and practices and the impact of these on women most at risk of being constructed as criminals. Chile's deep history of human rights violations, as well as ongoing legislative debates and recent gains to decriminalize abortion on three grounds—"when a woman's life is in danger, when there are fetal anomalies incompatible with life, and in the case of rape" (Maira, Casas, & Vivaldi, 2019, p. 121)—situated Chile as politically well timed to help reveal the impact of restrictive reproductive health policies on women.

Abortion in Context

Abortion is a personal and radical action within oneself. Reproductive health, including abortion, does not exist in isolation. The decision to terminate a pregnancy is unique for each person and often the result after weighing difficult

4 • *Introduction*

emotional, biological, cultural, social, economic, and/or political circumstances. Each woman's lived experience with abortion is specific to her. Eisenstein (2001) states, "[B]odies are always personal in that each of us lives in one in a particularly individual way. They are also always political in that they have meanings that are more powerful than any one of us can determine" (p. 1). To understand the complexity of women's diverse realities in Chile, I will highlight aspects of a few women's stories, Anaís, Constanza, and Paz,[2] to understand the context in which their abortion decisions were made.

Anaís was in her twenties when she had her four abortions. She already had a son with a partner she loved very much, and she saw her future with this man. But, during that pregnancy, it was a difficult time for Anaís because she was constantly fighting with her partner. She did not want to be pregnant and have a child, but she was in love with him, and he told her that he wanted to have kids. When she became pregnant, their relationship changed from one of freedom to one of responsibility. Her partner left Anaís and their baby to fend for themselves. Anaís never envisioned being or wanted to be a single mother. She went into a deep depression, which was the only episode of depression she has experienced. She framed this as going *"subterraneo"* (underground) and described it as an especially dark period in her life. As she was transitioning out of her depression, she had four pregnancies with three different men. The first of these pregnancies occurred because a condom broke. The subsequent pregnancies resulted from not using a condom because the men did not want to use them. In each instance she was clear that she did not want to have any more children, but forces beyond her capacity to navigate at the time ultimately resulted in another pregnancy. Her son was very little, and she was still recovering from the separation with her son's father. As a single mother she had limited income and was not in an economic position to have more children.

Constanza grew up in poverty. She was the daughter of a live-in domestic worker, and she was raised in the home where her mother worked. Growing up Mapuche in a non-Indigenous environment, Constanza faced racism from her local community. She also revealed that she endured daily physical abuse from her mother. She told me that the only time her mother did not hit her was on her birthday. Constanza was searching for a community to belong to and found it when she became politically active at an early age. This gave her a sense of identity and strength. She was a Communist for many years, involved with popular radio and various committees. Constanza had her first abortion when she was twenty-six years old, in 1990, the year that abortions in Chile became completely illegal. Although she was politically active, she was not involved with the women's movement, as she saw this movement as *"burgués"* (bourgeois). She was fighting for other causes, such as race and class equity. Neither was

Constanza's activism focused on women who faced violence in their relationships, even though she was in an abusive relationship that she labeled as "a crazy, insane relationship." Based on her experience, she shared that men do not understand, they are abusive, or they are not present: "you either feel love that is not there, or you do not have love." She tried to end the abusive relationship she was in many times, but it finally ended when he found out she was pregnant.

Paz was twenty-four years old when she had her abortion. At the time of the interview, Paz was twenty-six. When she became pregnant, she and her partner were unemployed and had been living inside their university during a *toma*.[3] Paz and her partner, like many other students during this time, were taking over and living inside their universities to demand free and quality education for everyone. The student movement was initiated by high school and university students and eventually became a conduit for broader "demands for structural change—such as nationalizing privately held natural resources, increasing taxes on the wealthy, and reforming the 1980 constitution imposed by Pinochet that was carefully designed to limit basic freedoms. . . . " (McSherry & Mejía, 2011, p. 29). Hundreds of thousands of people took to the streets to demand change. Some people I encountered on the street told me that they had not seen this type of protest for social change since the dictatorship of Pinochet. Paz disclosed, "It was really weird at that time because we were finish[ing] *la toma* . . . and we didn't have a house in that moment [because] we were [living] in the university . . . so we [stayed] at a friend's house." The friend she stayed with had a baby and Paz saw how important it was to be prepared to have a baby. Paz liked the idea of being a mom, but because of the political climate of the time, Paz did not want to have a baby. The struggle for equity in an unequal system filled her with a feeling of hate: "It's easy to hate on this planet with everything that is going on." She did not possess the confidence to bring a child into a context of struggle. Paz was upset that the government was not listening to ideas for positive change. Changing the educational system represented class equity, but with resistance from the government, she felt that they only wanted children as laborers, for the system, not unlike the discourse during the dictatorship. She asserted, "All children are welcome—for work." At the time of her pregnancy, they were just leaving the *toma* and she felt very "*decepcionado*" (disappointed) with the world. She questioned, "Why would I want to bring a baby into this situation?"

The three excerpts of Anaís, Constanza, and Paz do not represent the range of experiences the women interviewed shared about their abortion. Each woman voiced unique and personal circumstances. These narratives illustrate the context of gender, class, and race inequity in which their abortion decisions and experiences were embedded.

6 · *Introduction*

Criminalizing Women for Abortion

The discourse on the criminalization of abortion invisibilizes those who are most impacted by restrictive reproductive laws and policies. By centering solely on the act of abortion, the broader impact of criminalization on women's lives, experiences, and bodies is disregarded. This narrow perspective ignores the individuals most affected, reducing their visibility in shaping the discourse. Shifting the focus to the criminalization of women for abortion brings attention to the gendered consequences of harmful policies. Thus, reframing the criminalization of abortion as the criminalization of women for abortion is an intentional practice and politic to center women—and to use this as a guide to inform, understand, deconstruct, and produce knowledge about and practices to change harmful abortion policies that construct women as criminals.

Restrictive reproductive health policies disproportionately affect women and girls who are the targets of multiple forms of violence across the globe, such as poverty, gender-based violence, health disparities, and lack of educational and employment opportunities and access to needed resources, among others. The historic and oppressive systems that regulate gender norms and related inequity sustain complex layers of political, economic, and social disparities in which reproductive lives are embedded. Women often carry the brunt of being responsible for their condition, but they are not treated equally in their relationships, place of employment, or education and are often the targets of violence through discourse and exploitation. This, combined with lack of state resources and protection, on top of the multiple layers of discrimination against them, means that women living in poverty, especially, have little to no power to change the condition they are in. Under restrictive reproductive health policies, those who deviate from the construct of gender norms by terminating a pregnancy are criminalized. Laws and practices that criminalize women for terminating a pregnancy do not take into consideration the broader contexts of race, class, and gender inequity in which these laws are constructed (Mazza, 2011). To fully understand women's experiences with abortion in the context of illegality, considering the broader structures of inequity is critical, including the barriers women face in accessing health and economic resources. It is in this context that restrictive abortion legislation and its impact on women's reproductive lives need to be understood as reflective of the inherent inequity in social, economic, and political structures.

The illegality of abortion does not stop the practice or the need for abortion. In fact, the highest rates of abortion continue to be in countries with the most restrictive laws. Restrictive abortion laws produce two distinct phenomena, the construction of criminals and clandestine spaces. The social construction of laws and policies that aim to address social issues end up targeting specific behaviors, punishing individuals and communities with harmful consequences. This approach frequently fails to account for the unique experiences and exploitation of women, exacerbating their marginalization and reinforcing existing gender inequities, rather than addressing the root causes of the social issues they aim to solve. Laws that aim to criminalize specific behaviors simultaneously enforce public surveillance of marginalized populations. A personal decision to terminate a pregnancy becomes publicly scrutinized, fostering a discriminatory environment. When abortion is reduced to a crime, by which a woman is measured, she is stripped of her identity, sense of self and belonging, and the unique context of her decision. Thus, criminalizing women for abortion produces a narrow lens from which to understand the social issues surrounding reproductive health, rights, and justice. This leads to unjust and deliberate harm, as it unfairly assigns blame and responsibility to women. As a result, these women are burdened with unwarranted accountability for societal issues. Women criminalized for abortion are not only at risk of being arrested, followed by probation and/or prison time, but they also are forced to navigate a climate of discrimination, are invisible and vulnerable to abuse and exploitation, suffer serious health complications, and live in fear and isolation with no legal recourse or protection from the state. The context of criminality perpetuates internalized oppression and shame, impedes access to critical resources, sanctions marginalization, and disregards women's complex reproductive health experiences. The trend to criminalize women for abortion clearly reflects a race and class bias. The impact of restrictive reproductive laws and policies is most aimed at regulating the lives of women already marginalized in societies. The women who lack access to basic health and reproductive health care are the same women who are most harmed by restrictive abortion laws. These women are at higher risk of not only imprisonment without access to legal recourse, but also maternal mortality or serious health complications from obtaining unsafe abortions.

Unsafe abortion is one of the leading causes of maternal mortality worldwide, with the highest rates in the Global South. When abortion is illegal, it is forced underground, perpetuating unsafe and dangerous conditions for women, but it does not reduce abortion. The risks associated with having a clandestine abortion would be preventable if laws did not criminalize women, thus forcing them into precarious and illegal situations. Within clandestine spaces, the situation of illegality produces a black-market economy around abortion. Conditions to terminate a pregnancy are often unsafe and unhygienic, providers are usually not health professionals, and women are treated poorly and economically exploited without protection from the state. Specific to women living in poverty, the black market eliminates agency because they cannot afford to buy choice like other women with access to financial resources. Women living in poverty have no alternative but to put their bodies in harm's way, as there is no state regulation or protection of women in the black market. In this clandestine context, these women are silenced and invisibilized, and the violence and exploitation committed against them are state sanctioned.

Varying levels of legal restrictions on abortion are in place across the globe (Center for Reproductive Rights, 2023). As of 2025, forty-four countries make an exception to save the life of a pregnant person, forty-seven countries allow exceptions to preserve health, and twelve countries make exceptions based on socioeconomic status. In the seventy-seven countries that permit induced abortion with no restriction as to reason, policies are in place with a range of gestational limitations, as well as parental or spousal authorization or notification, among others. Within these four categories, multiple countries have additional legal indicators, such as permitting abortion in cases of rape or incest or in cases of fetal impairment. Twenty-one countries completely prohibit abortion with no exceptions, not even to save a persons life. Within the various categories of legal grounds, women continue to be at risk of being criminalized or having to navigate imposed restrictions that limit access to reproductive health care services. In addition, social, cultural, religious, health, and legal barriers make it virtually impossible for women to access safe abortions where restrictions are in place. Deep-rooted gender norms, perpetrated through patriarchal structures and practices, are revealed as lack of political will within various levels of government. Gender inequity, as it intersects with race and class, greatly determines women's reproductive autonomy, health harms, and risk of being criminalized for terminating a pregnancy outside of the legal grounds and cultural mores of a specific country.

The pro-choice/pro-life discourse on abortion in country-specific contexts does not reflect the complexity of abortion for women who are already navigating the challenges of inequity in multiple social and cultural situations. Understanding the broader context of inequity in which abortion decisions are made necessitates an examination of how we understand both *choice* and *life* paradigms. The *choice* paradigm does not include how women's agency is constricted when they are living in poverty, rural areas, or abusive relationships, for example, and do not have access to family planning, housing, transportation, income, or decision-making power. The *life* paradigm assumes that women who choose to terminate a pregnancy are not considering the life of others. However, the risk associated with having a clandestine abortion, such as threats to women's health and lives, is often juxtaposed with economic survival and parenting the children present in women's lives.

Women in the Global North and South have been connecting reproductive health and rights to human rights for decades, linking histories of colonialism and consequent restructuring of economic and political systems that undermine women's agency and reproductive sovereignty. Emerging out of the Black Women's Caucus at the 1994 International Conference on Population and Development (ICPD) in Cairo, reproductive justice[4] expands the limited pro-choice/pro-life paradigms of abortion as individual choice and responsibility by locating reproductive experience in a broader framework of social justice and human rights. This sheds light on the power that social, economic, and political constructions hold over individuals and communities regarding the human right to have a child under the conditions of one's choosing; to not have a child using birth control, abortion, or abstinence; and to parent children in safe and healthy environments free from individual or state violence (Collins & Bilge, 2020, p. 114). A reproductive justice framework highlights the underlying conditions, such as police/state violence, poverty, war, internal conflict, gender-based violence, removal of children, separating families, forced sterilization, sexual violence, incarceration, environmental exploitation, genocide, forced migration, and related constructions of racial, queer, immigrant, and disability injustices, among others, that govern abortion decisions and experiences.

Criminalizing women for abortion reinforces patriarchal oppression, in which a woman navigates the violence associated with gendered body politics. Consequently, in the context of abortion, marginality is a prerequisite for health harms and criminalization. The United Nations Special Rapporteur on the Right to Health (2011) addresses restrictive reproductive health laws and policies as a violation of the right to health. As a result, criminalizing women for abortion perpetuates disparities in health and justice, causing a deliberate violation of women's human rights.

Theoretical Framework

I began this study searching for a unifying framework to bridge macro and micro levels of analyses to provide a comprehensive understanding of women's lived experience being criminalized for abortion in Chile. This transpired into using several theories to design a multidimensional framework to help name and deconstruct the complexity of inequity while simultaneously centering women's narratives, linking broader constructs of violence to lived experience.

10 · *Introduction*

Using critical phenomenology[5] as an overarching framework helps to expand the phenomenological understanding of lived experience by including the structures of inequity in which these experiences are embedded. As reproductive lives are specifically shaped and regulated by social, economic, and political experiences, applying critical phenomenology offers a unique framework to bridge concrete and symbolic bodily experience with the context of broader structures of violence (Demello, 2014; Willen, 2007). The multiple constructions of inequity create the unjust context of women's reproductive health decisions and experiences. Thus, *violence* is an apt construct to make visible abstract and concrete harms of inequity toward women who are historically marginalized. Johan Galtung (1969), a Norwegian sociologist, introduced a typology of violence that includes structural, cultural, and direct forms of violence. These are not to be understood as disparate paths of violence, but rather as interrelated, multifaceted, and mutually reinforcing. Each provides an analysis independent of the other, but together offer a comprehensive look into the complexities of inequity, revealing a combination of various interlocking forms of oppression in which women navigate their reproductive lives.

Broadly, Galtung (1969) described violence as "avoidable insults to basic human needs" (p. 292). He argued that when harm is avoidable, violence is perpetrated. For example, hunger would be violence toward those who are starving, when resources are unequally distributed and there is a dearth of political will to address the issue. He further contended that structural violence is "built into the structure [of society] and shows up as unequal power and consequently as unequal life chances" (p. 171). A defining point of structural violence is that it happens over time rather than produced by a tangible episode of violence. In this way, structural violence is understood as a type of slow violence that is built into the system and becomes institutionalized. Farmer (2004) adds that violence is exerted systematically through historic economic and political structures and processes, which deny basic human rights to some while benefiting others. Structural violence is not the result of a mistake or an accident, but rather a conscious deliberation of social, economic, and political decisions over time that determines who will be harmed and who will be protected from harm (Farmer, 2005). To fully grasp the extent of structural violence, it is essential to critically examine the social, economic, and political practices rooted in settler colonialism. This involves analyzing how these practices perpetuate inequity and marginalization within societies. By exploring the historical and ongoing impacts of settler colonialism, we can better understand the mechanisms that sustain structural violence and the ways they shape the lived experiences of individuals and communities. Structural violence offers insight into the complex social construction of inequity, which constrains agency and violates human rights (Khan, 2014). Structural violence provides a framework to understand the reproductive laws, policies, and practices in Chile and how they create an unjust context in which women's reproductive health experiences are embedded.[6]

Cultural violence is defined as distinct elements of culture, such as religion, ideology, and language, that justify and legitimize structural and direct forms of violence (Galtung, 1990). This type of violence is expressed and perpetuated through attitudes and beliefs reflected in accepted cultural norms and dominant discourses. Galtung asserted that "culture preaches, teaches, admonishes, eggs on, and dulls us into seeing exploitation and/or repression as normal and natural, or into not seeing them at all" (p. 295). Thus, cultural discourse has the potential to be a conduit of permissive harm toward others, rendering subjugation and maltreatment as an accepted norm. Positioning harmful attitudes and beliefs as violence provides a powerful critique of the unjust realities experienced by the people most impacted. Where structural violence sheds light on laws and policies over time that constrict mobility and agency, cultural violence helps to explain how inequity is sustained through harmful discourses. In the Chilean context, identifying cultural violence and inequity helps to understand the significant role this violence plays in legitimizing and perpetuating harmful attitudes and practices toward women who have terminated a pregnancy. Harmful narratives dehumanize women, contributing to an environment where negative perceptions are normalized. Moreover, these cultural constructs influence legal and institutional responses, which lead to inadequate protections for women and a lack of societal accountability for the violence committed.[7]

The third classification in the typology of violence, direct violence, describes violence as visible through a direct personal link between the victim and the perpetrator. This type of violence is most recognized when we think of violence toward others. Galtung (1969) clarified the difference between direct (personal violence) and indirect (structural violence) as a person versus the structure of society as the perpetrator of violence. This reveals structural violence as abstract and thus more challenging to identify who or what entities are accountable for the violence committed, but it does not negate the direct impact that structural violence has on individuals and communities. For example, structural violence can be materialized on bodies in the way of hunger from poverty, disease from health disparities, or maternal mortality from abortion complications. Thus, direct violence is also the result of structural and cultural violence and cannot be separated from the other forms of violence in the typology. The in-depth interviews with women in Chile who have a history of terminating a pregnancy revealed how illegality is inscribed on a woman's body and embodied reality, linking broader constructs of violence to lived experience.[8]

Farmer (2005) added that race, class, and gender by themselves do not explain the forces that render individuals and groups vulnerable to human suffering. However, together they contribute an analytic lens to understand the complex ways in which human agency and potential are restricted. Restrictive reproductive health policies do not impact women equally, criminalizing women for not having access to resources or the ability to move freely within the limitations of their social location. The distinct forms of race, class, and gender inequity have deep histories, which construct the context of women's reproductive health experience. As Sutton (2010) has found in related research, "The fact that poor/brown female bodies are particularly likely to be injured or killed by dangerous abortion procedures exposes the criminalization of abortion as a form of classist, racist, and patriarchal disciplining of the body" (p. 193). Thus, a woman's vulnerability to the typology of violence is determined by her social location. Intersectionality,[9] therefore, is a critical addition to the model because structural, cultural, and direct forms of violence interact with race, class, and gender, among other social constructions of identity.

> Intersectionality investigates how intersecting power relations influence social relations across diverse societies as well as individual experience in everyday life. As an analytic tool, intersectionality views categories of race, class, gender, sexuality, class, nation, ability, ethnicity, and age—among others—as interrelated and mutually shaping one another. Intersectionality is a way of understanding and explaining the complexity in the world, in people, and in human experiences. (Hill Collins & Bilge, 2020, p. 2)

Intersectionality sheds light on the ways multiple systems of oppression are mutually constituted, resulting in distinct structures of and experiences with oppression. Intersectionality reveals that oppression manifests in unique structures and experiences, shaped by the interplay of multiple identities and social factors. Thus, in addition to highlighting broader constructs of inequity based on social location, intersectionality offers a pathway to understand and contextualize the unique experiences of women from diverse historically and systemically marginalized backgrounds.

Employing a multidimensional framework offers a comprehensive lens for unpacking the inequities that determine women's reproductive health experiences. By centering women and their lived experience, this approach holds space for the complexities of how structural, cultural, and direct forms of violence intersect and shape reproductive health experiences in the context of illegality.

Throughout the book, this framework will be used to emphasize the multiple forms of violence that women's reproductive health is embedded in, ultimately deepening our understanding of the challenges they face and underscoring the urgent need for a transformative response to support women's human rights and well-being.

Methods

Based on over a year of fieldwork in Chile between 2011 and 2014, this study examined the impact of restrictive abortion policies and practices on women in the context of inequity. This study shifted the focus from the criminal act of terminating a pregnancy to the women who are impacted by laws and policies that construct them as criminals. Using a critical phenomenological research design, an element of this research focused on the nature of inequity related to race, class, gender, and nation that exists within the context of local and global social, economic, and political processes around restrictive reproductive health policies. Semi-structured interviews were employed with various participants in academic institutions and legal, religious, health, feminist, community, and other nongovernmental organizations. The study was anchored in the narratives of women in Chile who have a history of terminating a pregnancy in restrictive and illegal conditions. This grounded the research in the narratives of women whose perspectives are generally devalued or ignored, offering a counternarrative to the harmful discourse on abortion. These in-depth interviews revealed how illegality is inscribed on a woman's body, bridging constructs of violence to lived experience. Women's narratives uncovered how their voice and experience with abortion are rendered invisible within clandestine spaces of illegality and are made visible only as a result of health or legal consequences. Despite the barriers women navigated within a highly criminalized environment, they revealed resistance to dominant cultural discourse and harmful policies, highlighting individual and collective forms of agency.

Connecting with women about their abortion stories seemed to unfold naturally in the field. Usually, the scenario developed with me sharing some aspect of my work and women opening up to me that they had an abortion. This came up unexpectedly, often, and in various settings, such as a town festival, protest marches, over coffee, in my living environment, and in a professional setting. Whatever the context, these conversations did not always end up in an in-depth formal interview. Many of the conversations I had with women about their abortion experience were unstructured and informal. However, field encounters were successful in a couple of different ways. First, they allowed women to choose whether to disclose their experience, even before broaching the topic of an interview. These women were not specifically approached to share their abortions with me. The decision to share was completely in their control. Only after they shared their abortion and rapport was established did I invite them to participate in a formal interview. Each of the women I approached in this way agreed to participate in the study. Another reason this strategy was successful in connecting with women was the rapport that was established during the informal conversations, so when the actual interview took place, it was not the first time we had met or interacted. This strategy helped to establish the formal interview from a deeper, more trusting place because it was not the first time women were sharing their abortion experience with me.

Observation and informal interactions in the field proved to be a valuable source of information for contextual data. I purposely scheduled my arrival in Chile to commemorate the 40th anniversary of the September 11, 1973, coup d'état. Having hands-on experiential learning opportunities gave me additional insights I would not have had through interviews. For example, while in Chile I participated in four marches: for the disappeared, with students fighting for equal rights and access in education, for workers' rights, and for the decriminalization of abortion. I attended various seminars on the decriminalization of abortion in Latin America, abortion and the protection of the unborn in the Chilean Constitution, the criminalization of abortion as a violation of human rights, health issues when abortion is criminalized, popular education in health, violence against women, and housing and community rights. I attended documentary film discussions on the U.S. involvement in the 1973 coup and a participatory mural project on the same issue. I attended a fundraiser for the Communist Party in a community that was heavily targeted by the coup, and a cultural dance performance in a *población*[10] north of Santiago's city center. I attended several cultural events in Mapuche communities in the south of Chile. And I participated in two workshops: a legal workshop regarding the rights and limitations of an abortion advocacy hotline, *La Línea*; and a women's art workshop in a *población* east of Santiago's city center. I visited sites of torture during the coup: Londres 38 (38 London Street) and the Gabriella Mistral Museum. I went to the Museum of Memory and Human Rights, walked around the presidential palace in the center of Santiago, *La Moneda*, to view the bullet holes that remained from the day of the coup d'état, and visited numerous women's organizations and *consultorios*.[11]

Just by living in Chile, I learned from the multiple interactions and observations in the field. I took public transportation and had many conversations with bus and taxi drivers, and other passengers, like me, while taking or waiting for

Introduction • 15

transportation. I saw the challenges for Indigenous people to access the public health care system while visiting my friends after a car accident and witnessed the corruption of the legal system as their rights were blatantly violated. I saw and felt the culture of *machismo* while traveling throughout Chile and through interactions with some friends and family members. I traveled between poverty and wealth, between repression and privilege. I had conversations with people who were extremely racist and others who internalized racism, as well as with many others who are fighting every day just to have a voice and a sense of belonging. I talked to people who were responsible for the harms committed during the dictatorship and others who suffered threats or torture or had a family member, friend, or neighbor who was murdered or disappeared. I talked to many single mothers who were working hard to be able to feed their children. I had conversations with young Bolivian women who crossed the border into Chile for economic opportunity. And I spoke with young women who were discriminated against in the public health care system regarding their reproductive health needs.

In total, forty formal, semi-structured and in-depth interviews were conducted with thirty-six participants. Twenty-five semi-structured interviews were conducted with participants affiliated with religious and academic institutions and legal, public health, economic, feminist, human rights, and community organizations. These interviews lasted between 45 and 90 minutes. Eleven in-depth interviews were conducted with women about their abortion experience. Four of the eleven women were invited for second interviews to delve more deeply into the phenomena being studied. These interviews lasted between 60 and 120 minutes. Interviews were digitally audio-recorded and conducted in both English and Spanish, depending on the participant's preference. I also had over sixty substantial informal conversations with diverse groups of people and hundreds of meaningful but more limited interactions, which consistently contributed to and guided the research.

I traveled within and across three diverse geographic regions: north, central, and south Chile. The northern region of Calama has a diverse population, including itinerant and local miners; the Quechuas, an Indigenous group from in Peru, Bolivia, Ecuador, Colombia, Argentina, and Chile; and a large immigrant population mostly from Bolivia, Peru, Ecuador, and Colombia. Calama proved to be an important geographic area to understand issues of ethnic and gender inequity, specifically for immigrant women. Like many areas in Chile, this region has a clear class divide between rich and poor. Despite the differences between Santiago, Viña del Mar, and Valparaiso in the central region, in the outskirts of each of the city centers are *campamentos* and *poblaciónes*, communities of houses that were constructed over time by families, often as a politic act, through *tomas* (land takeover), on public or private land due to the lack of housing available for people with little to no income. Some of these communities are over fifty years old, so the houses and infrastructure have been constructed over the years and are well built, as you might see in the city centers. However, many of the communities in the outskirts of Viña del Mar and Valparaiso are still isolated, without an infrastructure of paved roads, water, or electricity. These communities offered an invaluable understanding of the economic, social, and geographic marginalization of women who live in these areas. The southern region of Temuco and the surrounding area are the heart of the Araucanía Region, one of Chile's poorest regions and home of the largest Indigenous population in Chile, the Mapuche. Throughout history, this area has been exploited for its natural resources, to the detriment of the local Indigenous population. Visiting this area was critical to understand the experiences of inequity, specifically of Mapuche women. The focus of attention in the three regions contributed to a contextual understanding of spatial differences of inequity. This added a profound richness, which spoke to the differences and similarities of women most marginalized in Chilean society: immigrant women, young women, women living in poverty, and Indigenous women.

Positionality and Reflexivity

The nature of conducting research brings up dynamics of power indifference and politics of representation (Sultana, 2007). Mullings (1999) states, "we embark upon research with maps of consciousness that are influenced by our own gender, class, national and racial attributes" (p. 337). Knowledge therefore is shaped by and interpreted through one's social location. Thus, ethical research is sustained by the practice of critical reflexivity throughout the design, implementation, and analysis of the research (Sultana, 2007). In developing and conducting international research, being aware of my positionality was key throughout the entire research process. Although my family is from Chile, I am a white-presenting cis woman born in the United States, and although I grew up in a low-income household, I am now university educated, with a working- to middle-class background, and English is my first language. Most Chileans are a mix of European and Indigenous backgrounds, but often, lighter skin is associated with a higher class. I had the mobility to move in and out of privileged spaces of race and class that others did not. On the other hand, because I am the daughter of immigrant parents from Chile and my extended family lives in various areas of Chile, I am familiar with the language, culture, and politics, which aided in developing relationships.

While conducting international fieldwork in Chile, it was especially important that I was cognizant of my international positionality in relation to the United States' history of economic and political hegemony in Latin America. The involvement of the United States in overthrowing Allende and supporting Pinochet throughout the dictatorship was a theme that came up during some interviews and field interactions. As a researcher from the United States, sometimes I was being questioned for my motives of doing research in Chile. Other times it felt as if I were being blamed for the harms committed during the dictatorship. It is critical to recognize that at times I was seen as representing a global power entity. The United States' history of imperialism throughout Latin America made understanding my place of privilege in relation to some of the participants and field interactions crucial. I found it important to listen and hold space for others to have questions and critiques of the United States and my role in Chile. Only through using these strategies would the dynamic shift to a working relationship and understanding of mutual respect of like politics. Sultana (2007) states, "similarities and differences that emerge through the relations that are involved in the research process [demonstrate] the ways that alliances and collaborations can be forged. . . ." (p. 380).

Sutton (2010) speaks to research, politics, and solidarity becoming interrelated while in the field. As a woman with my own histories of violence and intersectional identities, I felt personally connected to other women who shared their stories of isolation, discrimination, and strength and resistance. Though my politics frequently aligned with others regarding inequity in Chile, I do not claim to generalize what will unfold in the sharing of these stories. Through an ethical commitment to and honoring of the people who shared their lives with me, my aim is to highlight the stories that unfolded in hope of raising awareness of what was revealed. This includes examining the relationship between restrictive reproductive health policies, inequity, and the construction of criminality, as well as the impact on women's lived experiences; the importance of centering women to guide our understanding of abortion in the context of inequity and illegality; and how a multidimensional framework to deconstruct inequity can move us toward the realization of just reproductive policies and practices and women's human rights.

CHAPTER 1

Inequity

A Social Construction

> We don't own our bodies . . . it is very evident in
> respect to your body that it is owned by the state.
> —Emilia, a social worker in the south of Chile

Laws and policies that shape women's reproductive health in Chile, including abortion, have been influenced by the specific international and local political climate of the time. Narratives of the participants interrelated with the historical context of reproductive laws and policies illustrate the impact of structural violence on human experience, locating bodily connections to local and global processes (Anglin, 1998; Khan, 2014). This chapter reveals how reproductive health policies and their changing impact on women can be situated within three specific time periods, each in part influenced and guided by global phenomena. The first of these, pre-1973 coup d'état, introduces a health framework that addressed abortion in the context of social medicine and Cold War overpopulation discourse. The next, during the seventeen-year dictatorship between 1973 and 1990, illustrates how anti-Communist sentiment and neoliberalism shaped a generation of repressive and restrictive policies. The last, the return to democracy from 1990 to 2014,[1] explores the conflict between the aftermath of Pinochet's population policies and the introduction of human rights discourse, which sustained inequity for women already marginalized in society and gave an international platform to advocate for women's reproductive rights and the decriminalization of abortion, respectively.

20 • CHAPTER 1

Pre-1973 Coup d'état

The introduction of social medicine in Chile prompted a movement to implement policies that addressed rising health issues because of poverty. The roots of social medicine in Chile date back to the mid-nineteenth century, but it became more established in the 1920s and 1930s, in part due to the social impact of heavy migration to the city centers and subsequent demands of the labor movement (Waitzkin, 2001, p. 1593). In the late 1930s, Salvador Allende, a physician by training and then minister of public health, published *La Realidad Médico-Social Chilena* (The Chilean Medical-Social Reality), an analysis of the impact of social and economic conditions on the health of the working class. His work was considered cutting edge, as he incorporated other issues that had not been emphasized previously, such as infant and maternal mortality and illegal abortion. Allende (2005, reprint) framed the issue of infant mortality as a problem of "illegitimacy"[2] and poverty, as single mothers lacked financial resources. According to the Civil Registry in 1938, about 30 percent of children were born to single mothers. These births accounted for almost 50 percent of infant deaths.

In the early 1930s, there was a major change to Chile's abortion policy. From 1874 to 1931, abortion was considered a crime in all cases, but in 1931, a health law was implemented that gave doctors authorization to provide abortions to save a woman's life (Human Rights Watch, 2009). According to Waitzkin (2005):

> Allende gave one of the first analyses of illegal abortion. He noted that a large proportion of deaths in gynaecological hospitals, about 30%, derived from abortions and their complications. Pointing out the high incidence of abortion complications among working-class women, he attributed this problem to economic deprivations of class structure. (p. 740)

By the late 1930s, Allende was framing abortion as a public health concern due to inequity. He recognized the causes of health disparities rooted in inequity, so he continued to organize for just health policies, with a specific emphasis on maternal and child health care. In the 1950s Allende was instrumental in developing universal health care access. And in 1966, Chile had developed neighborhood health centers (NHC), later called *consultorios*, which were generally located in *poblaciones* (Waitzkin, 1983). At this time, each NHC was responsible for providing services to 50,000 to 75,000 people within a specific geographic area. By the 1960s Chile had developed one of the most progressive reproductive health programs in the Americas. With financial support from the United States, which saw poverty as counter to economic development in Latin America, Chile was able to respond to the high rates of maternal mortality from unsafe abortions by implementing a state-subsidized family planning program (Casas, 2011; Moenne, 2005; Shepard & Casas Becerra, 2007).

The Cold War and population control paradigm were two parallel, albeit intersecting, dominant discourses that motivated the creation and implementation of U.S. President John F. Kennedy's *Alianza para el Progreso* (Alliance for Progress) in 1961. The *Alianza para el Progreso* was designed to contain Communism through promoting capitalist development and "democracy" in Latin America over a ten-year period with the promise of economic growth, equitable income distribution, and the alleviation of poverty, hunger, and illiteracy through promoting housing, health, and education (Faúndez, 1988; Kennedy, 1961). The possibility of a democratically elected socialist government in Chile was of the greatest concern to U.S. foreign policy during this time, so money was allocated to Chile under the guise of repelling Communism (National Security Archive, 2004).

In 1962, U.S. aid to Chile through the *Alianza para el Progreso* totaled nearly $200 million. By 1970, this figure had grown to $1.5 billion, combining aid from the U.S. government and international agencies with significant U.S. involvement. During this period, Chile ranked second only to Vietnam in the amount of U.S. aid received (Michaels, 1976, p. 77).

Under President Frei (1964–1970), Chile used some aid from the *Alianza para el Progreso* to develop a comprehensive nationwide family planning program, in part as a strategy to tackle overpopulation, which the Global North framed as leading to the spread of poverty and Communism, interfering with global progress and economic development (Pieper Mooney, 2009). Hence, "as part of the population control paradigm that shaped the postwar world, medical and political elites [in Chile] reevaluated the meanings of motherhood for the body politic" (p. 69). Consequently, women's reproductive bodies were positioned as subjects of state control.

In addition to population control, Chile's progressive reproductive health policies during this time were driven by the high rates of maternal mortality from unsafe abortion. Many medical professionals were operating within a framework of social medicine and subsequent protection of women's health. Numerous studies conducted in the 1960s on abortion helped to shed light on abortion being a major public health issue in Chile (Armijo & Monreal, 1965). Between 1940 and 1965 the rate of abortion increased by 104.4 percent (Pieper Mooney, 2009). In 1960, about 60,000 women were hospitalized for abortion complications and only a third of the women hospitalized for post-abortion care in the early to mid-1960s left the hospital alive (Armijo & Monreal, 1965; Pieper Mooney, 2009). As Alejandra, a feminist at a nongovernmental organization (NGO), recalled in an interview with me, "At that time there were high death rates for women due to reproductive causes, especially clandestine abortion."

Women living in poverty were most at risk by unsafe abortions. These were the women who were being hospitalized and dying because of clandestine abortions. Pieper Mooney (2009) documents the high-risk abortion procedures used during this time as the insertion of "unsanitary rubber catheters, tubes, wires, sticks, or plant stems into the uterus" (p. 55). Francesca, a community member in a *población*, recalled that women with little to no income relied on using knitting needles, or a *sonda*, which was a rubber tube placed in a woman's cervix for two or three days, a technique participants explained was given only to women with limited resources. These methods were more likely to produce infections that put women's lives at risk. Francesca said that of the women she knew, at a minimum, they lost their uteruses.

Francesca continued by conveying that women in the *poblaciones* were systematically excluded, in part because they lacked access to contraceptives or their birth control methods failed. Some women's partners prohibited them from using contraceptives in the context of a violent relationship. Abortion is an extreme measure that women take only when all else has failed. These women were exploited, neglected, excluded, and marginalized in both the home and the state. Women were at risk because of the intersection of inequity and illegality. Francesca recalled, "Death from abortion is the greatest injustice there is because nobody should die through the process of . . . abortion. The practice of abortion is very simple, it is not a complex issue, but here [if] women are forced to continue with pregnancies, they die."

Many physicians grew deeply concerned about the harms associated with the abortion epidemic in Chile and became staunch supporters of family planning initiatives (Pieper Mooney, 2009). This led to the medicalization of contraceptive technologies through intensive research, mostly conducted on "poor" women: "women became part of studies for the sake of medical advancement and the development of new technologies" (p. 57). Francesca remembered that women from impoverished backgrounds were used as guinea pigs for new forms of birth control, later to find out that some of these forms of birth control produced cancer in women. For some women from lower-income areas, this generated distrust in the public health system. I found this level of distrust still reflected in women's experiences when visiting outlying *poblaciones* and *campamentos*.

Due to the research on reproductive technologies, the first intrauterine device (IUD) was created in Chile in 1959 (Pieper Mooney, 2015). Isadora, an activist at a feminist NGO, stated, "because maternal mortality was very high, Chile started with the development of contraceptives . . . the Copper-T was created in Chile [to] make intervals between the pregnancies and to reduce pregnancies." According to Pieper Mooney (2009), in 1966 Santiago "gynecologists inserted IUDs at rate of sixty devices a day" within a population of 460,000 (p. 61). This became the preferred method of birth control for many women in Santiago, including in the low-income and working-class sectors. Between 1964 and1969, birth rates decreased by 33 percent.

Through developing and implementing a state-subsidized family planning program in the 1960s, contraception was made widely available in public health clinics and hospitals, with a target goal of reaching 15 percent of the female population of reproductive age (Casas, 2011). In the early 1970s, during the Allende administration, this program added sexual education as well as public health outreach to 40 percent of the population, which included women who had a history of clandestine abortions (Casas, 2011; Moenne, 2005). These efforts were successful in significantly reducing abortion and maternal mortality rates.

Pía and Rocío, two participants who spoke about their reproductive experiences in the early 1970s, demonstrate distinct experiences of women who benefited from the discourse during the Allende administration. Pía remembered a health clinic as part of the University of Chile in Santiago in 1970 that offered access to free birth control: "I remember at the university my right to get the *anticonceptivos* [contraception] absolutely free in 1969." Rocío, a woman from a *población* in Santiago, went to a clandestine clinic in 1973 and had an abortion with the *sonda* technique, the typical method for "poor women." At that time she was still able to check herself in to a public hospital for three days to be monitored for potential complications without the threat of being arrested. Rocío's story highlights the emphasis on health versus criminalization when addressing issues of abortion for women during the early 1970s.

Although health during this time was often framed as connected to social and economic issues and allowed for the development of universal health care access, Pieper Mooney (2009) suggests, the focus on women, especially low-income women, further constructed the "unfit mother," thereby increasing state surveillance and limiting women's agency (p. 29). Thus, women's bodies and reproduction have historically been situated at the intersection of the broader constructs of inequity and social control. Further, the focus on reproductive

24 · CHAPTER 1

health was never about women's reproductive rights, in part because a consciousness of equality for women had not yet developed. Paola, a feminist researcher, explained:

> Of course if we look at that time, as good leftists in my experience, women's issues were not the most important, they were absolutely hidden because we were talking about [class] equality [but] . . . gender issues had no existence, not only for us, but also for political leaders. . . . If you read the speeches of Allende, it's incredible because he says, "all you women, [you] will be starting at the university, you will be a professional tomorrow, but you will have to go now and help women with the children" . . . a woman's place is very clear, it's a very traditional place. How this changes, I would say that after the first land reform of Frei and then with Allende, there's a lot of explosion of social demands, but they have no gender dimensions at all.

Although the main emphasis at the time was on class, not gender issues, Isadora believed the ideal was to "solve all discriminations and dominations [with] class first and then gender."

According to Casas and Herrera (2012), family planning policies during the 1960s were aimed at reducing maternal mortality from unsafe abortion, but not "intended to liberate women from the burden of raising a large number of children so that they would develop as individuals. Then, family planning was not considered a right" (p. 142). Thus, giving contraceptive access to women pre-coup d'état was in response to the Cold War and overpopulation discourse to tackle poverty and to combat maternal mortality, but not to support or increase women's reproductive rights. Despite lacking a gender equity lens during this time, reproductive health policies were successful in lowering abortion and maternal mortality rates, and they situated abortion within a health rather than a criminal paradigm.

Dictatorship: 1973–1989

Just as the Cold War discourse constructed women's reproductive experiences pre-1973 coup d'état, it equally generated ideological manifestations of control during the dictatorship of General Augusto Pinochet. Under Pinochet's *Política de Población* (population policy), a pro-birth policy was implemented, "linking the development and defense of the nation to the size of the country's population" (Moenne, 2005, p. 156). When I asked Francesca her thoughts on Pinochet's population policy intentions, she talked about manipulation and control, "because the government wanted more pregnancies, more children. I say cheap labor, we said to ourselves [in the *población*], to exploit more people."

Inequity • 25

According to Pieper Mooney (2009), "attention to gender roles, to women's maternal responsibilities . . . proved critical in the consolidation and maintenance of authoritarianism" (p. 7). Aiming to control the masses of political activity, the military subjugated women to traditional roles within the home. A familiar discourse emerged that limited women's role to that of mothers and wives. Pinochet's wife, Lucía Hiriart Pinochet, was instrumental in promoting the importance of family to the nation-state. The rhetoric often included talk about women's inborn responsibilities and self-sacrificing service to others (p. 135), without a reality base of what was happening for many women. Paola recalled that women in underserved communities had to recreate themselves during the dictatorship. She reflected:

> I think it's interesting to read the speeches of Mrs. Pinochet because they had all these great organizations for women in the idea . . . of the good mother, the family, this woman that's full of virtues, see, it's interesting to read about that because that's a speech, but what's happening with women, it's so different, the reality, because the men are unemployed, they have to go away to work, [women] have to deal with every problem, and they have to build themselves again in this context.

According to Pieper Mooney & Campbell (2009), "many families could hardly function in an environment shaped by sudden military raids, curfews, and ongoing arrests" (p. 8). Mercedes, an activist who lives in a *población* north of Santiago's city center, remembered that no one was allowed to leave their house after five o'clock, making it very difficult for those who lived on the outskirts of Santiago and worked late or had to travel by bus to get home before the curfew. Francesca, who lives in a *población* east of Santiago's city center, recalled that traveling during this time was dangerous because the military could stop you at any time and question you. Francesca remembers the military surrounding the *población* with tanks in the street and helicopters circling overhead, which Ani said occurred during the first weeks and months of the dictatorship.

There were significant political and class distinctions between the ideology of women's responsibility to the nation-state and the reality of the people economically marginalized in Chile, who were suffering what Sepúlveda (1996) describes as a double repression, being the recipients of both state terror and the economic and political restructuring in the country (p. 14). As part of the Chicago Boys Chile Project, privatization increased, drastically cutting public spending (Klein, 2007). Education and health were the sectors most impacted, with women living in poverty experiencing increased barriers in health and reproductive health care. Luisa, a social worker from a health organization in a *población* south of Santiago's city center, spoke to the issue of privatization as an issue of injustice:

26 · CHAPTER 1

> You realize it is a systematic plundering of the public . . . it was a very smart way to transfer funds to the private and dismantle the public. So that's the problem that is being delivered in . . . a system that was generated to accumulate profit from social services. Before, the state guaranteed . . . the common good. It's a little picture that makes inequity in the country . . . immoral.

Between Pinochet's population policies and the increase of privatization, the state-subsidized family planning program was dismantled. Isadora remembered contraceptives being removed from public health clinics within two to three years after the coup. She had heard multiple stories from women in impoverished areas who used to have access to the pill, for example, and then it was no longer offered. In addition, programs and educational resources provided in public health clinics as part of the family planning awareness campaign were removed, as well as the comprehensive sexuality education programs that were developed in 1972 to address teen pregnancy (Casas & Ahumada, 2009). Isadora remembers when the sex education programs that began under Frei were taken away: "they burned all the [sex education] books . . . everything was burned and disappeared. Then we had 17 years with nothing in the schools . . . especially for the poor sectors." Isadora is addressing the unique impact on public spaces during the dictatorship. Public institutions, which low-income and working-class populations used, were censored by the military and therefore were most impacted by restrictive policies.

Further, under Pinochet's dictatorship, public health facilities were under surveillance of the Dirección de Inteligencia Nacional (DINA, National Intelligence Directorate), the state's secret intelligence, which was tracking women who had abortions (Moenne, 2005). Public health facilities were mandated to report any woman who came in for post-abortion complications. Eighty percent of the reports documenting women who terminated their pregnancies during this time originated from public hospitals (Center for Reproductive Law and Policy, 1998). Women who lacked economic resources were most at risk of being arrested because they depended on public health facilities when faced with complications from terminating a pregnancy in illegal conditions (Casas-Becerra, 1997; Center for Reproductive Law and Policy, 1998; Vargas, 2008).

Because of the fear surrounding the criminalization of abortion, women suffered from more severe health complications. Ani explained, "It was bad news from a public health point of view where you were seeing women coming very late into hospitals and perhaps with more serious health consequences." Thus, a criminal paradigm did nothing to stop the need for abortion or save women's lives. A criminal paradigm only reinforced the clandestine nature of abortion and the stigmatization and isolation for women who were seeking to terminate or had terminated their pregnancies. Francesca recollected a story that happened in her *población*:

> Once, we went on a bus. I was young and there was a woman standing in a bus stop. The people said [to the bus driver], "Hey, stop, stop, stop, why don't you stop?" [The bus driver said], "Not if that bitch had an abortion," and the woman, I saw, the blood was running down her legs. I remember she had a dress [on] and the blood ran down her legs and the [bus driver] said, "No, that bitch had an abortion." I was a girl, very young, but things leave you . . . marked.

This story not only highlights how attitudes about abortion are internalized in the general public's consciousness, such as Francesca's statement about being *marked* from her experience as a witness, but it also speaks to the marginalization that occurs for women who have had abortions. Galtung (1990) describes marginalization as a component of structural violence, in which exclusion is a major factor. In addition, a factor of marginalization is not having choice, which was reflected in this woman's experience at the bus stop and will be reflected in the next example given.

The lives of low-income women were specifically regulated by reproductive policies and practices during the dictatorship. Isadora remembers the forced removal of women's IUDs in public health facilities. She had interviewed women from under-resourced neighborhoods at the time and they told her that their IUDs were removed without their consent. Francesca also remembers stories of women in her community who had their IUDs removed without consent. She shared that women who were over forty-five years old were becoming pregnant because the health clinic had removed their Copper-T. Francesca never had an IUD forcibly removed without her permission, but she found out what was happening in talking with other women in the *población*. One woman was pregnant at fifty, and Francesca was told that this woman had her IUD removed in the *consultorio*. Women did not want to go to the *consultorio*, because they did not want their contraceptive devices removed. Many women in the economically disadvantaged sectors were trying to regulate their own reproduction, as they already had more than two or three children and did not want any more, in part because of the impact of the economic restructuring during the dictatorship. Francesca said, "There was a time for women when they didn't want to get pregnant because they didn't want their children to die of hunger and this also happened during the dictatorship." This exemplifies how women experienced inequity, illustrating the divide that was amplified between women with limited resources and women who had resources. Women who lacked financial

28 · CHAPTER 1

resources had limited agency concerning their bodies. Many participants reiterated that violence comes from not being able to exercise the right to make decisions about their own bodies.

Preventing women from using *anticonceptivos*, such as through removing their IUDs, left women with very few options to control family planning. Thus, the pronatalist policies under Pinochet gave women no options but to resort to precarious methods, often putting their own lives at risk (Martinez, 2013). For the two participants who terminated their pregnancies in the early 1970s, their political reference and personal experience were distinct from those of other women interviewed. Pía and Rocío had access to *anticonceptivos* as a result of the 1960s public health campaign and were not shaped by the rhetoric under the military policies during the dictatorship. This created a unique experience for them, as they did not express levels of stigmatization in the same way as the other participants who terminated their pregnancies after the return to democracy in 1990. One only needs to look closely at the difference between public health policies of the 1960s and the 1980s in Chile to understand how the social construction of laws and policies had a marked influence on defining women's reproductive health experience.

Return to Democracy: 1990–Present

Between 1931 and 1989, it was legal, although not always the practice, in Chile to obtain a therapeutic abortion to save a woman's life under section 119 of the Health Code. However, in the last weeks of Pinochet's dictatorship in 1989, after seventeen years of military rule, Pinochet changed this law, making all abortions illegal (Casas-Becerra, 1997; Htun, 2003; Rayas, 1998; Vargas, 2008). Section 119 was amended, stating, "No action may be executed that has as its goal the inducement of abortion" (as cited in Abortion Policies: A Global Review, 2002, para. 2). The Catholic Church played a significant role in shaping and influencing political and gender norms in Chile throughout history (Casas, 2009; Shepard, 2000). Alejandra, who works at a feminist NGO, asserted, "the church had a fundamental role in this restrictive policy around abortion." During and after the transition to democracy, the Catholic Church had been committed to restricting women's reproductive health and rights (Shepard, 2000), isolating "abortion as an assault on motherhood, sex roles, and the origins of human life" (Htun, 2003, p. 151).

Twenty-eight years[3] after Pinochet repealed the 1931 Health Code, abortion laws in Chile remained among the most restrictive in the world; they contained no legal exceptions to terminate a pregnancy, not even to save a woman's life

(Casas-Bercerra, 1997; Htun, 2003). Following the return to democracy, multiple laws had been proposed to either liberalize or further penalize abortion, but these were either archived or rejected until recently (Casas, Vivaldi, Silva, Bravo & Sandoval, 2013). In 2015, a bill was introduced to decriminalize abortion in three circumstances. In 2017 the Act on the Voluntary Termination of Pregnancy (VTP) was adopted. This bill legalizes abortion on three grounds: to save a woman's life; in cases of rape or incest; or fatal fetal impairment (Casas et al., 2022). This historic decision was not reached without considerable effort and challenges, and it still has yet to be realized in practice.

SHIFTING PARADIGMS: 1990–2014

In the years after the return to democracy, the government had softened its emphasis on directly criminalizing women for abortion, compared to this practice in the 1970s and 1980s under Pinochet. Participants attributed this shift to multiple factors. Some stated that the political climate change from dictator to democracy was instrumental in creating space for public discussion to return to universities and feminist and medical organizations about reproductive health and rights. Further, Isadora explained that during Michelle Bachelet's appointment as health minister in 2000, "she started opening the door for what today are reforms that made possible to have a law that supports reproductive rights and access to [the] day after pill." Alejandra cited the shift as linked to the publicized cases of pedophilia within the Catholic Church. This instilled distrust in the messaging from the church and in turn helped to shift cultural attitudes toward the decriminalization of abortion in certain cases. Further, decriminalizing women for abortion was achieved through feminist mobilization,[4] as well as the unwavering activism and advocacy of women within legal, health, and academic institutions, among others, who continue to highlight the social, economic, and political systems that undermine women's autonomy and their ability to make decisions about their reproductive health.

In the 1990s, women's reproductive rights were getting more international attention. 1994 marked a turning point for international discussion on population policy at the International Conference on Population and Development (ICPD) held in Cairo (Ashford, 2004). Whereas pre- and post-1973 coup, population policy was focused on controlling population either through providing access to or the removal of family planning services, respectively, the discussion post dictator included talk on enhancing women's social development and empowerment, with access to family planning as part of women's overall health and well-being. In addition, in 1995 the Fourth World Conference on Women in Beijing included addressing unsafe abortion as a violation of women's human

30 • CHAPTER 1

rights and a major public health concern (UN Women, 1995). Surprisingly, Pinochet signed the Convention on the Elimination of All Forms of Discrimination Against Women (CEDAW) in 1980, and it was ratified in 1989, a few months before his departure as dictator (Walsh, 2011). This was the same year Pinochet made performing all abortions illegal. By this time Pinochet had shifted his view of women from one as self-sacrificing mothers contributing to the nation-state by way of their reproductive bodies to one of women as responsible for contributing to the nation's economic development. The incongruence between signing CEDAW and eliminating any safety net for women by making abortion completely illegal was most likely due to mollifying both the neoliberal economic actors and the Catholic Church.

Pinochet's legacy of restrictive reproductive health policies continued after the transition to democracy. Women continued to put their lives at risk as a way to manage their reproduction. Thus, the shift to decriminalize women for abortion also came from the negative health consequences that doctors themselves were observing (Casas, 2011). Under military policy in the 1980s public health practitioners were mandated to report women who came in for abortion complications. The shift in public health policy not to report came from specific providers within the medical establishment. Ani recalled having conversations with doctors in the Ministry of Health who, over time, realized that criminalizing women for abortion was bad policy, "from a public health perspective, criminalizing women is a health consequence."

BARRIERS TO ACCESS

While I was in Chile, it was obvious that the struggle to recognize reproductive rights for women in Chile was far from over. Framing and understanding abortion in a much broader context of health reveals multiple barriers. Women who are economically disadvantaged continue to bear the brunt of policies that restrict access to, and the quality of, health and reproductive health care. Luisa, a social worker in a *población* where 90 percent of the population relied on the public health system, explained the problem with *consultorios* as in both the structural design and the implementation of services. In 1998, 89 percent of women of reproductive age were being screened for cervical cancer through the Papanicolaou test (Pap test). This was due to a public health campaign that allowed for such high rates of women to be screened. However, in more recent times, Luisa said that in any *consultorio*, no more than 40 percent to 60 percent of women are screened for cervical cancer, which is very low. This produces serious problems, in both the absence of early cancer detection and the impact on the health of women who were initially detected with cancer. When women do not return to the *consultorio*, the cancer continues to advance. Referring to the *población* in Santiago where she works, Luisa lamented, "and this is what happens in the sectors that are most discriminated against and most abandoned." Luisa credits the high rates of cervical cancer in economically disadvantaged women to inequities embedded in the public health care system. There is a lack of political will at the state level to distribute the needed resources to *consultorios*, which results in a lack of information, lack of prevention efforts, and limited hours that do not work for the people who live in the *población*. For example, *consultorios* close between 5:00 p.m. and 7:00 p.m., but most of the women in her *población* do not return home until 8:30 p.m. and often work on Saturdays.

> *Consultorio* hours [do not] permit women to do Paps. . . . And we are in such an exploitative system where women cannot get permission [to leave work] for their exam because they miss so much time when their children are sick. . . . It's much more difficult for women who live by themselves with their children without a partner [and] who do not have [another] provider [in the home].

Another issue that participants described related to both the *consultorio*'s location and its configuration. Maria José lives in a *campamento* in the steep hills of Viña del Mar. The *campamento* was made up of over 1,000 families but was first created through a *toma*.[5] Historically, a *toma* has been part of political resistance. The dwellings in the *campamento* where Maria José lives began with the construction of shack-like structures with corrugated metal siding and roofs. Over the years people have made additions to their homes, and eventually most of the structures became well-developed houses. However, the community still lacks infrastructure, denoting the difference between a *campamento* and a *población*. In many areas, there is no electricity, no inside or outside lighting, and no running water. Throughout the community are unpaved roads, most of which are on extremely steep hills, eroded over the years by the rains. This makes it virtually impossible for vehicles without four-wheel drive to travel, such as cars, taxis, buses, and ambulances. Maria José told me it takes about 45 minutes to walk down the steep hill to get to the bus stop and then another hour, more or less, by bus to reach the *consultorio* for their area. Maria José reflects:

> Yes, it's far and a sacrifice because everyone [has to] go to the bottom and after to the top. For example, here there is a woman who carries her [disabled] daughter in her arms to the bottom . . . then she has to carry her back up. This is a sacrifice because the daughter is heavy, but what is she to do when nothing goes up, not even an ambulance.

Maria José continues by sharing that sometimes an ambulance arrives at the bottom of the *campamento* in a specific location, if the driver knows the road, but mostly it is difficult to give directions because there are no road signs, only a maze of dirt roads. The ambulance often gets lost, "almost more than half a day lost," she continued. "These are the limitations when you have to live in the *campamento* at the top of a hill," especially when it rains. Deep crevices in the road turn into small creeks when it rains. This makes it difficult for trucks to travel on the roads. Maria José said that people often slip in the mud and fall down. This is the case when bringing children to school, going to work, or going to the *consultorio*. Women have to arrive to the *consultorio* very early in the morning to put their name on a waiting list, only to wait hours to be seen by a *matrona*. To further complicate matters, it is often dark while these women are trekking down the hillside. All these issues are barriers to access for women with limited economic resources who are relegated to receiving care in the *consultorio* designated to their area.

Being limited to receiving care in one *consultorio* was also an issue for teenagers, who rarely went to *consultorios* for contraception for fear of running into their neighbors. Fernanda explained:

> I think that happens with very young people, that maybe they start having sexual activity, at, I don't know, 14, and they could go to the *consultorio* to ask for pills or something . . . but they don't do it because they will go and maybe the neighbors are sitting right next to her waiting for the dentist and they will see her waiting for the *matrona*, so they don't want that to be so public.

Adolescents over fourteen years old have a legal right to access contraceptives in a *consultorio*, but because of the social pressure of being discovered by someone who can identify them, they do not go. In part, this is because of the way that *consultorios* are designed. For example, in Fernanda's *consultorio*, there is no system in place to protect confidentiality regarding what services someone is there to access.

> So, if you go to the dentist you will be sitting outside the dentist office, if you go to the *matrona*, you will be there and the *matrona* will open the door and say, "Juanita Perez come here," so . . . [in] the waiting [area], you see every[one] that is in the *consultorio*.

Francisco, a psychologist in the north of Chile, said it is the same at the *consultorio* where he works. "The parents are very conservative, they care about that, so kids don't want adults [to] know that they come here for contraception, no, no way." In addition, in 2004 Chile modified its statutory rape law to include mandated reporting on any teenager under fourteen years old who was sexually active (Casas & Ahumada, 2009, p. 89), which proved to be an additional barrier for adolescents to access contraceptives. This law targets mostly girls from low-income areas, because they depend on the public health system for access to reproductive health care, so it perpetuates health inequities.

Many participants spoke from professional and personal experiences to the unique structural barriers immigrant women face within the public health system. These women are confronted with state policies that restrict their mobility and access to resources. A large portion of immigrants living in the north of Chile live in Calama, home to the biggest open-pit copper mine in the world (Jarroud, 2015). The immigrant population in this region is mainly from Bolivia, Peru, Ecuador, and Colombia. While traveling in the area, I conducted one formal interview with a woman from Ecuador and five informal interviews with women from Bolivia, whose ages ranged from early twenties to early thirties. All but one traveled to Calama by themselves in search of work opportunities. These women often are at risk of violence and economic exploitation and are forced into sex work. I met a young Bolivian woman, Johanna, who was working at the hostel where I was staying. She shared that she had come to Calama to make money and that she felt lucky because she found good employment with a good boss. She had met many women who were not so lucky and were forced into prostitution. Still, her situation was unstable. She overstayed her tourist visa by five weeks and needed to return home to visit her three children she had to leave behind. She was worried about crossing the border after violating the stipulation of her visa.

Johanna's story is just one of many. Immigrant women face a plethora of issues: fear, depression, exploitation, abuse, loss of leaving their families and children behind, and lack of state support and protection. At a Catholic church that I visited, the sisters provided an array of support services to immigrant women, including spiritual and maternal support, holding space, creating community, and providing resources and referrals. Sister Maria emphasized that undocumented women constantly face social and economic difficulties. The challenges that undocumented women of reproductive age faced also showed up in the lack of access to services, high maternal and infant mortality rates, dependence on relationships that are violent and exploitative, and lack of state protection. Alma shared that immigrant women face constant discrimination, racism, poverty, and abuse within a system that is designed to marginalize and serves as the context in which reproductive health is both limited and controlled.

Although the most recent iteration of abortion policies in Chile decriminalized abortion in the three circumstances—to save a woman's life, in the case

34 • CHAPTER 1

of rape, and in cases of fatal fetal impairment—the discrepancy between law and practice remains one of the biggest challenges moving forward. Legalizing abortion does not immediately change cultural attitudes and beliefs, which are needed to realize pregnant people's right to abortion as part of overall reproductive health care. Multiple issues continue to act as barriers to implementing abortion in practice. Lack of awareness about the law in general and rights that exist within the law; institutionalized race and class bias; the stigma and fear experienced by women seeking abortion, as well as abortion providers; lack of political will by the state; unrealistic time limitations; and conscientious objection by medical providers, among others, continue to interrupt women's right to health, which includes abortion (Biggs et al., 2019; Casas et al., 2022).

Conclusion

Abortion has not disappeared throughout Chilean history. However, women's experience with abortion has shifted depending on the specific political climate of the time. Each of the three time periods has been influenced by global factors, such as social medicine, U.S. aid, the Cold War, population control ideologies, neoliberalism, public health, and human rights. These developments suggest that Chile's reproductive health policies are situated within a global and historical context that have determined women's reproductive health experiences. Some shifts in policy and practices have been positive, such as the progressive reproductive health policies pre-1973 coup d'état, and the inclusion of human rights framing after the return to democracy, and more recent decriminalization of abortion. Despite this progress, economically marginalized women have been the target of reproductive policies throughout history by the relentless inequity entrenched within Chilean society. Participant narratives confirm the ways these women have been most harmed, reiterating that women's bodily experience is situated at the intersection of the broader constructs of inequity and social control. Economically underserved women have been used as guinea pigs for new reproductive technologies, they have been forced to have children in the context of extreme poverty and violence during the military regime, and they are constant targets of criminalization when they deviate from the construct of acceptable gender norms. It is not a surprise, therefore, that these women lacked trust in the public health care system.

The theoretical construct of structural violence elicits a distinct way of discerning inequity as a visible and systematic harm toward others. Structural violence helps to shed light on how human experience differs within the same social, economic, and political system depending on a woman's race, class, gender, and national identity. However, structural violence alone does not explain how implementing progressive reproductive health policies does not improve equity in and access to quality health care for economically disadvantaged women. Historic and systemic in nature, systems of inequity are further sustained and legitimized through cultural discourse, which effectively limits women's agency and makes oppression and injustice invisible and normalized, and thus more difficult to address.

CHAPTER 2

Unpacking Inequity

> There is nothing wrong with underlining personal agency, but there is something unfair about using personal agency as a basis for assigning blame while simultaneously denying those blamed the opportunity to exert agency in their lives.
>
> —Farmer, 2005, p. 29

Cultural violence, like structural violence, is the result of historic processes, which contribute to dehumanization and marginalization in social, economic, and political spaces (Mullen, 2015). Through laws, policies, and practices, structures of inequity are legitimized and normalized within a sociocultural environment. Cultural violence makes it difficult to change repressive systems, as it reinforces and gives permission to treat people as less than human, often directly harming segments of the population constructed as *other*. Structural, cultural, and direct violence are interrelated and mutually reinforcing. This chapter explores how cultural violence fosters a permissive environment of discrimination and related forms of direct violence against women. The discussion will focus on the dominant cultural discourse and how it is sustained and normalized through multiple intersections of oppression, including race, class, and gender injustice, emphasizing distinct experiences of groups within the context of historic and systemic inequity. This chapter delves into the manifestation of cultural violence as a barrier to reproductive health, examining the role of discrimination, individualism, and *machismo* as contributing factors. The way that cultural violence sanctions harmful treatment of women is uncovered through historic and contemporary constructs of violence against women.

Fernanda, an occupational therapist who works at a *consultorio* in a low-income area of Viña del Mar, described Chile as a paternalistic culture, suggesting

38 · CHAPTER 2

that social hierarchies are rooted in a subordinate culture of control. In exploring this further, she explained that this dynamic has been going since colonial times. "There was a very, very high distance between the *patrones de terrateniente* [landowners], like the people in charge, the boss, and *obrero* [worker], the people who worked in the countryside a long time ago." She added that people with less power have historically been forced into submission, and this is reflected in both policies and practices. Fernanda further describes this level of submissiveness as embodied in people's consciousness, making it difficult for people living in poverty to advocate for themselves around their health issues. So, even though people may have a right to health, they do not always exercise this right. Fernanda added:

> I think it's the responsibility of us, that sometimes maybe [the *consultorios*] do not give the information, "you have a right" . . . so it's lack of information from us to the people and a passive paternalist culture on the other hand.

Trumper (1999) describes Chile's paternalistic culture as being rooted in a hacienda system imposed over hundreds of years following Spanish colonization. It was a powerful system in which the *patrones* ruled over the workers and their families, demanding total obedience and submissiveness. In addition to the *patrones* representing the economic elite, they also dominated political and legal arenas. *Patrones* had their own police force, and each *patrón* for a specific area acted as the judge. Further, due to the social construction of race, class, and gender, "the white Spaniard had the right to rape, control, and dominate the conquered native women" with total impunity (p. 7). Thus, race, class, and gender inequity have been central to the dominant cultural discourse in Chile since the imposition of colonial systems.

Chile's history of race, class, and gender discrimination did not begin with Pinochet but was harshly reinforced during the dictatorship. As part of transforming Chilean society and promoting a neoliberal agenda, the military initiated a systematic reign of terror against individuals considered a threat (Bruey, 2009; Richards, 2005; Sepúlveda, 1996). Thousands of people were arrested, tortured, disappeared, or exiled. The Mapuche, Chile's largest Indigenous population, lost much of their land that had been restored to them during the Allende administration, forcing many Mapuche women to migrate to the urban areas to seek employment as domestic workers (Richards, 2005). *Poblaciones* were heavily targeted with *allanamientos* (raids), systematic and repeated armed searches that resulted in violent home invasions, detentions, and interrogations (Bruey, 2005; Sepúlveda, 1996). To legitimize perpetrating violence against impoverished communities, the military government established after the coup labeled people as Marxists and Communists, a threat to the new restructuring of a neoliberal economy. Further, during the dictatorship, sexual violence was widely practiced as a form of torture and punishment, but it was heavily silenced (Moenne, 2005). Women were not considered victims of state repression but rather deviants of social norms. Last, Pinochet's population policies enforced the arrest and imprisonment of women for abortion (Casas, 2011; Moenne, 2005; Center for Reproductive Law and Policy, 1997). This emphasizes the extensive suffering experienced by individuals belonging to marginalized racial, economic, and gender groups within the context of a repressive military regime. This regime has been pivotal in perpetuating a present-day atmosphere of discrimination against Indigenous communities, economically disadvantaged people, and women, among others.

Racial Injustice

The official language of the Mapuche is Mapudungun. *Mapu* means earth and *che* means people, so the Mapuche are the people of the earth. The Mapuche are the largest Indigenous population in Chile, and occupy the Araucanía region in the south of Chile. Since the arrival of the Spanish, the Mapuche have been struggling to protect their ancestral lands, first from the Spanish starting in the 1500s and then from the Chilean state after Chile gained independence from Spain in 1810 (Richards, 2010). Under the Chilean state, the Mapuche were heavily targeted with violence and forced to live on *reducciones* (small parcels of land), which made up only 6.4 percent of their original lands. This was part of the state war of extermination in 1883 called the *Pacificación de la Araucanía* (Pacification of the Araucanía). European immigrants were recruited to occupy the surrounding territory, which produced an inherent conflict that exacerbated the marginalization of the Mapuche people and favored people of European descent. The historic mistreatment of Indigenous people set the stage for ongoing racial discrimination. Throughout history, the Mapuche people have been deliberately and continuously subjugated. There was a time during the Allende administration when agrarian reform policies redistributed land to the Mapuche, but the Pinochet regime refused to recognize the Mapuche and instead privileged corporate rights by both outlawing and privatizing Mapuche communal lands (Culliney, Peterson, & Royer, 2013). To date, Chile is the only remaining country in South America that does not recognize Indigenous groups in its constitution (Cultural Survival, 2019). To further restrict Indigenous rights, under Pinochet's 1984 Anti-Terrorism Law, Mapuche people who fight to protect land rights are at risk of being criminalized. According to Richards (2010), "the law allows for indefinite detention of suspects without charge, permits prosecutors' use of wiretapping and protected witnesses to whom the defense has no access, and authorizes sentences longer than those for similar violations of the civil code" (p. 74). It was not until 1993, a few years after the return to democracy, that the Aylwin government passed the Indigenous Peoples Act, ensuring the right to participation, rights to land and development, and cultural rights. Despite this, the anti-terrorism law remains in effect to this day (Culliney, Peterson, & Royer, 2013).

Indigenous communities throughout Chile continue to face the highest levels of poverty and illiteracy (Cultural Survival, 2019). These enduring challenges contribute to their isolation and exclusion and the perpetuation of harmful stereotypes, discrimination, and individual and state-sanctioned violence. While I was traveling in the south of Chile, a woman who owned the hostel where I stayed made derogatory and racist remarks against the Mapuche people. Conversely, on each of the bedroom doors in the hostel were wood signs of words in Mapudungun, such as *antü* for sun, *küyen* for moon, and *mapu* for earth. In the same town of Temuco, a woman working at a women's development agency asked me, "Do you only want to learn about Indigenous issues with women? Because it's complicated here." She looked around, lowered her voice, and stated that Indigenous people receive a lot of benefits, yet there is an ongoing desire for more. These examples underscore deeply ingrained systemic and institutional racism, which profoundly shapes the experiences of Indigenous communities. Temuco is considered the heart of Mapuche country, but when the Mapuche attempt to reclaim their rights, others who hold more power and privilege in society project an authoritative superiority. For example, the woman at the hostel said that when Indigenous people are quiet and tranquil, it is "peaceful," reiterating submissiveness as an accepted and expected cultural norm.

Constanza, raised by her mother who was a live-in domestic worker, lived in two worlds—one with a lot of protection and care in the home of her *patrona* (employer) and the other, which was her reality in Chilean society. Constanza was harmed by multiple systems related to poverty, gender, and race/ethnicity. The internalization of the racist messages and the violent treatment she faced had a profound effect on her sense of self growing up. Internalized racism embodied within individuals often produced subsequent disembodiment of identity, separating themselves from their Indigenous roots and identity. Rayen, a Mapuche woman who works for an Indigenous development organization, stated:

> The worst violence is discrimination, racism, because this starts with nothing, with race, only by looking at someone's face. Race is another concept that

intersects in the body. Mapuche are very heterogeneous because there are distinct colors of skin . . . a mark of race very distinctive and that's significant.

The historic struggle for land rights has instigated much state-sanctioned violence against the Mapuche. Rayen explained that there are historic documented cases where the Mapuche were physically marked, like animals. More recently three youth, Matías Catrileo, Alex Lumen, and Carlos Curinao (Unrepresented Nations and Peoples Organization, 2008; Zibechi, 2009), were killed "like animals" by a special police force. In an attempt to suppress the Mapuche's efforts to reclaim their ancestral lands, there has been a significant increase in indiscriminate state violence against Mapuche communities, prompting human rights organizations like the United Nations Children's Emergency Fund (UNICEF) to condemn the militarization of Indigenous communities in Chile. This violence has caused an unfortunate number of unintended casualties among those not directly involved, who had become targets of the special police force. Estrada (2009a) reports:

> Mapuche villagers have reported, for example, that a 14-year-old boy who was collecting herbs for a traditional healer in the village of Rofue was forced onto a police helicopter, taken aloft and threatened with being thrown out unless he confessed to taking part in a land occupation. (para. 12)

In the community of Temucuicui, made up of about 120 Mapuche families in the Ercilla region, police fired pellets and tear gas canisters into a school, wounding several children. Other children suffered respiratory problems. While in the south of Chile, I discovered that the surrounding communities of Ercilla were heavily militarized. In fact, on two separate occasions I was told it would be difficult for me to visit these communities without having an inside contact. One man I met at a grassroots human rights organization in Temuco asked me if I had documentation, because the police checked all documentation of anyone coming or going. He said if I was not a local, the police would not let me enter and could confiscate my U.S. passport. These communities were completely isolated, blocked off from any outside help or support to witness human rights violations, not unlike the time during the dictatorship.

Mapuche women have been visible actors in these struggles, participating in defending ancestral sacred territory through land recuperations, protests, and marches, among other forms of resistance (Richards, 2005). For many Mapuche women, their gender is intertwined with other parts of their identity, including race and class. The challenge arises when issues or intervention approaches are framed as individual, rather than collective. Mapuche women who identify as feminists do not always identify with Chilean middle-class feminists, because their issues are not being understood or voiced in their entirety. Rayen explained that within the Mapuche worldview or cosmovision, there exists a collective identity closely linked with nature, often conflicting with the more mainstream individualistic perspective that emphasizes individual behavior. She explained that when a community has a direct connection with nature, you are connected to your body. For example, Mapuche women do not have the same type of shame regarding bodies that comes from the west and from religion. Mapuche women have a distinct form of connection and relationship to their bodies. Rayen reflected, "Because we are integral, the body is part of us, [and with] racism and discrimination, you leave your body." She discussed how different systems such as health and education do not value culture but are more geared to separate one's identity, including the body, from that person, treating their body as separate from the collective, from the earth, and from their natural ways of being in the world. Because of this view, many Mapuche women do not seek care in public health clinics, such as *consultorios*. The imposition of individualism acts as a potential barrier for Indigenous women in accessing health and reproductive care. Rayen felt that reproductive health policies are backward, in that you need to have knowledge of your body to ask for and advocate for services. Rayen emphasized that when the body is part of the collective, "*no hay una preocupacion por uno*" (there is not a concern for the self). For example, Mapuche women do not speak about their rights, but rather the rights of the pueblo, which includes their families and children. Thus, for Indigenous women, the vision and services of *consultorios* are fragmented at best. Services are not integral, and this disconnect creates a barrier to care.

Cultural attitudes that place value on a population, which render them *somebodies* or *nobodies*, as defined by Trumper (1999), determine a permissive level of dehumanization and exploitation. The experience of inequity in Chile is multidimensional. Indigenous and immigrant women who live in poverty are distinctively harmed by historical systems of oppression based on race, class, and gender, which limit or deny opportunity.

The immigrant women I interviewed endured explicit racism, including instances of verbal and physical mistreatment by their employers. Francisco pointed out that the arrival of Afro-Colombians in Calama, in the north of Chile, marked the first time local Chileans had encountered people of African descent. Thus, this population of immigrants was regularly the target of discrimination by Chileans and other immigrants, with women being stereotyped as either drug traffickers or prostitutes, constructing further social and economic marginalization.

In the mining town of Calama, prostitution plays a significant role in the economy. This phenomenon results from the convergence of traditional gender roles, limited opportunities for women, and the exploitation of women within a well-organized capitalist sex work industry. As described by Rojas (2012), certain areas in Calama are designated as moral zones. These moral zones are condemned by middle- to upper-class Chileans. Francisco explained that the downtown area is a sex work moral zone. Locals know about and talk about the area, but they say they do not go to that area, which is not true. Moral zones are portrayed as frequented by outsiders, but Rojas revealed in his study that this is a social belief not grounded in actual practice. Moral zones are typically frequented by local Chileans, yet the responsibility for perceived social issues is often attributed to immigrants, specifically immigrant women. According to Shepard (2006), this is a double discourse, where individuals promote "traditional and repressive sociocultural norms publicly, while ignoring—or even participating in . . . these norms in private" (p. 15). Upon further investigation, I found that most sex workers in Calama are Chileans, while most immigrant women migrate to Calama to seek employment in the service sector. Nevertheless, a hierarchy of inequity persists within the sex work industry, with immigrant women being the most vulnerable. Alma explained that in the sex work industry, there are two distinct groups. The first group comprises women who have dedicated their lives to this profession, who are typically employed in venues where sex work is practiced, such as in a *choperia,* or "café with legs." Most of these women are Chilean and have received some level of college education. The second group consists of women who have not completed basic education. These women entered the workforce at a very young age, and as a result, often have limited or no literacy skills. Within this group is a higher percentage of immigrant women. Francisco recalled a woman he worked with at the *consultorio*:

> I used to have a patient of mine, a very poor woman, she tells me, "I don't have money to pay the water services or the electricity," so one day I was driving in my car in the night . . . and I saw her in the street. That was the most shocking thing that ever happened to me with a patient . . . it was hard for me to see her there because I know that woman does that because she doesn't have money to live, for survival. She wasn't doing that because it was her choice. And in the street, it is very dangerous and they earn very [little] money.

The interconnected and hierarchal systems of oppression, such as race, class, and gender, profoundly shape a woman's agency within multiple contexts, including the realm of sex work. Immigrant women who are perceived as outsiders not only face accusations of contributing to the perceived moral decline of an

44 · CHAPTER 2

area, but also find themselves pushed into a less privileged position within the sex work industry. This marginalization puts them more at risk of experiencing violence and unintended pregnancies.

Class Struggles

Chile consistently shows up as one of the world's top-ranked countries with the greatest gap between rich and poor. Racism, classism, and sexism are interrelated and deeply embedded in contemporary cultural attitudes and laws because of the historical structures and processes that have shaped the nation. Paola shared that inequity has been continual in Chile's history. She stated that disparities between Mapuches and Chileans, the rich and the poor, and women and men have been accepted as "normal." However, inequity is not normal; it is the normalization of inequity that is the issue. Normalizing inequity is not unique to Chile but rather a representation of how cultural attitudes and beliefs can sustain systems of inequity. This manifests in distinctive ways, including the restriction and denial of opportunities within multiple systems, such as employment, education, and health.

The laborers I met, such as carpenters, electricians, and painters, were Indigenous or immigrants with limited financial resources. They were extremely underpaid, if paid at all, but highly depended on to build and improve Chile's infrastructure. Pablo, an economist from an NGO, stated that workers fighting for unions are stigmatized. Leftover from the Allende/Pinochet ideological conflict between socialism and neoliberal capitalism, many businesses are seen as not functioning properly if they have a union, he stated. Moreover, a recurring theme emerged in multiple discussions regarding the significance of last names. If an individual possessed a Mapuche last name and was equally qualified for a job as someone with a European last name, the person bearing the Mapuche last name would not get the job.

Specific to domestic workers who work outside of the home is a cultural expectation that they do not neglect their household duties. Paloma, an immigrant woman from Peru, began her workday at 6:00 a.m. and did not return home until 7:30 p.m. As soon as she got home, she took on her own household chores of cooking, cleaning, and washing her children's clothes until 1:00 a.m. As a domestic worker, Paloma cared for other women's children as well as her own. This scenario is not unique. Immigrant women like Paloma faced economic exploitation across different geographic regions throughout Chile. Many women I met shared their stories of being required to exceed their maximum work hours or give up their days off, especially when they were live-in domestic workers. The lack of time off made it nearly impossible for these women to access health care, including reproductive health services. In Paloma's case, her employer warned her that getting pregnant would result in losing her job, which she relied on to support her four children.

Public education is another significant issue that perpetuates and reinforces systems of inequity and stereotypes about people from low-income backgrounds. The prevailing structure of the public education system is a direct result of the privatization of education under Pinochet (Espinoza, 2008; McSherry & Molina Mejía, 2011). Privatization reinforces class structures. Only lower-income students receive public education at the primary and secondary levels. Anyone who can afford to pay attends semi-private or fully private schools. Many people I spoke with from the low-income sectors reiterated that the quality of education is vastly different between the public and private systems, in large part because state resources allocated to the public education system are lacking. Francisco spoke about the educational system as a system of exclusion and marginalization, which reinforces segregation between the lower class and the upper class. This segregation restricts exposure to different classes only within the confines of the *patrón/obrero* roles that have existed for hundreds of years. In Francisco's experience, he explained:

> Education doesn't help too much because the opportunities for a kid that is studying in a public school are very little. We are a very segregated society in all ways . . . they don't trust each other, so people who are in the low class are more resentful to people that are in the high class and the high class doesn't trust the people [who are] in the low. So, social mobility is almost non-existent in Chile. . . . I don't think that happens . . . there [are] very few poor kids that get to a university, get a career, and get out of the poverty cycle.

Alma pointed out that educational inequities are tied to economic and social inequities. If women do not have a technical or professional career, they not only have less access to health and reproductive health care, but also, this makes it difficult for women to emerge from poverty. The cycle of poverty is reinforced through the privatization of education; thus, classism is inherently built into the system, which enforces the normalization of inequity. Marta, who works at a feminist health organization and grew up in poverty, talked about the impact of the public education system:

> I feel that in one way, we are marked by our context. The issue of social class is more concrete . . . because people who are poor do not have a chance to decide what they want. Education allows for a place of experience. With family in a situation of poverty, of precariousness, [one's experience] is conditional on

46 · CHAPTER 2

> where you were born and from there to be able to move forward. The potential for change is minimal. I think that education is indeed a possibility, but also a possibility that requires economic resources. So above everything, education is what places a barrier on us.

These existing structures of inequity shape women's lives and serve as the context in which reproductive health choices are limited and controlled. Emilia, a social worker in the south of Chile, explained that women who are economically disadvantaged have very little right, in practice, to exercise choice or decision-making. "We don't own our bodies . . . it is very evident, in respect to your body, that it is owned by the state," she explained.

Gender Inequity

Throughout Chile's colonial history, race, class, and gender norms have been strongly reinforced by the Catholic Church. During the Spanish colonization, particularly within the structure of the hacienda system, women were expected to maintain a continuous labor force through reproduction (Trumper, 1999, p. 7). In Latin America this has been reinforced through *machismo,* the attitudes, beliefs, and societal norms of what it means to be a man, and *marianismo,* which defines women as self-sacrificing wives and mothers. Both *machismo* and *marianismo*[1] are rooted in the religious construction of the power of men over women and the submission of women to men, respectively (Cianelli, Ferrer, & McElmurry, 2008). *Machismo* as a cultural expression encompasses a wide range of beliefs, behaviors, and attitudes that historically have been rooted in the social construction of masculinity, often legitimizing violent and unequal power and privileges. Within binary gender constructions, women are treated as subordinate to men, and motherhood is seen as a hegemonic form of feminine embodiment (Center for Reproductive Rights, 2010; Sutton, 2010). Womanhood and motherhood are so strongly associated that many people I spoke with shared that it is hard to imagine a woman without being a mother. During a conference I attended, one of the panelists raised this concern. She was requested to introduce herself and provide information about her marital status and whether she had children. This fosters cultural discrimination toward women by reducing women merely to the roles of wives and mothers.

Machismo proved to be a major barrier for women to access reproductive health care. Participants spoke of partners or husbands who refused to let women go to the *consultorio* to access *anticonceptivos.* Women shared that to legitimize their status as men, their partners or husbands wanted to have many children. In this context, men controlled women's reproductive health, and they often did so with violence. Alma asserted that a woman has a right over her own body, but often the husband does not agree, because "they have a jealous relationship that is violent." Many women who attend Alma's *consultorio* do not tell their husbands that they are there to receive birth control, for fear of retribution. *Machismo,* as a control mechanism to limit women's agency about their reproductive health, was also represented in structural ways. For example, while still in Peru before she immigrated to Chile, Paloma wanted her tubes tied, but the medical facility would not perform the procedure because she was still fertile and of reproductive age. To have her tubes tied, she needed permission from a male member of her family, which no one was willing to give, so she could not have the procedure. *Machismo* limits women's choice and agency. For Paloma, her life was not her own. In fact, when discussing her identity, she said that she did not identify as a woman, because her identity as a woman was defined by a man. Her self-defined identity rested in motherhood. I thought this was interesting considering that the social construction of women's identity as mothers also limits choice and agency, as discussed previously. However, for Paloma, being a mother saved her life, because her children were the strongest force in her fight to survive.

Divorce has been legal in Chile since 2004, much to the chagrin of the Catholic Church, which stated that divorce would threaten the stability of marriage and the family (Ross, 2004). After the return to democracy in 1990, there was an effort to pass legislation in support of women's rights, such as protections pertaining to sex discrimination, sexual assault, marital property, and divorce (Blofield & Haas, 2005). The first bill in support of divorce, presented in 1991, referred to individual rights, but it was considered too contentious to debate (p. 57). Bill 1759, introduced in 1995, reframed the divorce law as a mechanism to strengthen families. This bill incorporated multiple restrictions, such as "a mandatory five-year waiting period . . . and judges were given broad powers to deny divorce requests . . . [making] divorce much more difficult to come by" (p. 58). However, the church dominated the opposition to block this legislation through heavy lobbying and television campaigns (Ross, 2004). "[T]he Chilean church insisted that Catholic legislators could not promote policies that contradicted church teaching" (Blofield & Haas, 2005, p. 59). Bill 1759 was finally passed in the Senate in 2004.

For many women, divorce was a way out of violent relationships, but it did not come without a struggle. Paola spoke to the discrepancy between ideology and policy:

> We do not have a divorce law until 2004 and we have a violence law in 1994. Imagine what that means, how could you go and demand the husband for violence if you cannot get divorced? See? I remember no one could understand

48 · CHAPTER 2

what was the logic of the political program for women in Chile if they did it that way. And why is it that way? Because there was some pressure from the feminist movement for a violence law, but for the government in the 1990s, I remember . . . you could not speak about divorce . . . you could not write "divorce research."

The Catholic Church held a lot of political power after the return to democracy. In the 1990s, the church was influential in sustaining a moral culture of expected norms. I had one conversation with an elderly man, a father of grown children. Each of his children had been divorced, and I asked him if it was difficult for him. He responded with disappointment, "You hope that you instill good morals in your children," signifying divorce as *bad* or *wrong*. He seemed worried about what other people would think of him having divorced children. In this way, the choices of his children reflected his gender and class status. Thus, cultural norms are systemic in nature, which is why they carry so much power and potential harm.

The inequity of women's reproductive health has been reinforced by the authority of the Catholic Church (Casas, 2011). The church often denounces sexual behavior outside of the institution of marriage, thereby limiting needed education and resources. Lack of sexual education and prevention education in general was a concern for different professionals who work with sexual and reproductive health. Luisa shared that information regarding prevention and intervention is one of the most deficient areas of public policy. She added that policies with a vision of diversity are missing:

> It is an element which may be stated discursively, but not operationalized . . . and there is lack of resources allocated for effective care of diverse populations because resources are for basic care and there is no incorporation with what is really happening. . . . The structure of the population is changing today . . . there are older people in need of care . . . more pregnant adolescents with family problems . . . and the [issues] of the gay, lesbian, and trans populations are invisible.

As a result of the Catholic Church's condemnation of sex, discriminatory attitudes continue to circulate in the general population as well as in the health sector. For example, due to moral objection, adolescent girls are sometimes denied the morning after pill. As Isadora stated:

> We have a lot of road still to walk . . . it's definitely a struggle, you know, it's everywhere. And you know that the church, the changes in the church have a tremendous influence. Now, for example . . . they have their own universities, and they are preparing decisions and those decisions are saying they don't accept the modern contraception, and they don't want to give the prescriptions too . . .

we have some areas that don't allow the after day pill in their municipalities, it's incredible. We're in the middle of the struggle. We have a lot of things to do still.

This highlights the influence of the Catholic Church on the political and social landscape. The Catholic Church is a dominant force in defining lived experience for women in Chile, specifically around reproductive issues. The lack of separation between church and state allows the Catholic Church to exert its authority over reproductive self-determination (Northrup & Shifter, 2015). This not only limits women's agency but also fosters a highly criminalized and discriminatory societal environment that harms women.

Tamara, who works at an NGO in Chile, shared her struggle navigating her Catholic upbringing and her advocacy for reproductive rights. Growing up, she was taught to regard contraceptives as a type of abortion. She faced significant inner conflict with the concept of abortion, because of how she internalized the messages from the Catholic Church, which she shared as "very backward, hierarchical and *machista*." The messages she received characterized women who had abortions as "bad, criminals, murderers, sinners." At one point she thought she was pregnant, and she found herself with only two options: going against the Catholic teachings and having an abortion or having another child, which she did not want. This was a very difficult struggle for her. Every night she lay in bed not knowing what she was going to do. She recalled, "I lived how the majority of women lived . . . with my head full of thinking I was bad and of my Catholic teachings." Tamara's problem was not economic; she could have had three more children. Her issue was that she did not want any more children. She admitted that for other women with no resources or money, it is more difficult. She had the means to seek medical assistance for an abortion, but fear held her back. She realized through her experience that "the vision on the other side is completely distinct" and that it was impossible to know what someone else was going through. Tamara expressed, "I am a good Catholic now, thanks to God . . . before I was a bad Catholic because I judged a lot." Before she felt righteous in her ideology because she believed in God. She explained:

> But fortunately, I changed. I opened my eyes because the other reality, I had never seen before. So, now from my experience, I believe it is very important to demonstrate to others, the other side, to put the shoes on of women who have aborted, because it is not easy.

Tamara felt that the general public thinks abortion is easy, and if abortion were legal, then everyone would have an abortion. Mainstream media repeats the

50 · CHAPTER 2

same rhetoric: "if abortion was legal, all women would have abortions." Tamara added:

> It's on the radio, on the TV, in the schools, in conversations, [it's] the dominant cultural discourse on abortion. And in the Catholic schools they cycle the same information, that abortion is bad, it's a sin, women are criminals who kill, who kill children, they're not embryos, or fetuses, they're children. So, it's complicated.

Paola described a family member who was pregnant with a fetus who had major deformities and would not survive. This woman continued with her pregnancy because she was Catholic and believed in the dominant discourse of abortion as murder. Minutes after she gave birth, the baby died. Paola described her cousin's experience as shaped by a cultural narrative that equates abortion with killing. Paola reflected:

> Why does society criminalize something? I don't understand. I think it's the moral of the church, of the religion. It's the only reason why we associate, as a society, [to] criminalize pregnancy . . . and to feel that you don't want to have a baby. . . . Why [do] we have to feel bad about something very human, it's totally human.

Francisco characterized abortion as invisible in society, saying that people acknowledge its existence but choose to avert the reality. He attributed this partly to the societal expectations surrounding motherhood, making it challenging to envision a woman defying gender norms and expectations. He explained that it is difficult for Chileans to visualize a woman making a different choice, not to want a child or become pregnant, because they have another purpose in life.

Criminalizing women for abortion emerges from the moral control that both religious institutions and government policies exert over women's reproductive lives, generating harmful societal attitudes toward women who have had abortions. Women often are criticized, dehumanized, and relegated to the margins of *other*. In response, Paz shared that women are separated by a system that puts them on one side or the other: "Are you a good woman or a bad woman?" She continued, no matter what side you are on, the system does not want you to find each other, keeping women isolated.

INTIMATE PARTNER VIOLENCE

According to the Center for Reproductive Rights (2015), in 2013 the National Prosecutor of Chile reported 24,000 cases of reported sexual violence against women, of which 74 percent were under the age of eighteen (para. 2). Many participants discussed the violence from men toward women in Chile as endemic. Across all geographic areas in every community that I visited, the topic of intimate partner violence (IPV) emerged. This included physical, verbal, and sexual abuse. Although these types of violence are direct forms of violence against women, they are a product of and interrelated with structural and cultural violence. Direct violence is embedded within broader structures of inequity, as Muñoz Cabrera (2010) highlights: "women's exposure to violence is related to their position in the multiple systems of inequity and shows a tendency to increase as these systems intersect, creating layers of discrimination and exclusion for different types of women" (p. 10). Therefore, IPV must be understood not simply as harmful actions but as a consequence of unequal power dynamics within social, economic, and political systems that restrict the rights of women.

Throughout Chile's history, violence against women has been present, but it was not until the late nineteenth century that cases of violence began to be legally documented. This period marked the end of conflicts in the north and south regions of Chile and the beginning of the Chilean state. Gabriella, a university student, conducted a study regarding violence toward women from court cases in the Araucanía region between 1900 and 1950. She focused on intimate partner violence toward economically disadvantaged women from the country as well as Mapuche women. At the time of the interview Gabriella found 300 cases out of thousands that pertained to this type of violence. The documented cases showed that women received injuries from knives and sticks, endured rape and incest, especially young girls, and were often kidnapped. There were also cases of murder. Limited documentation showed perpetrators being held accountable for their crimes, indicating a climate of impunity that has upheld a system of gender inequity.

Luisa highlighted the most pronounced expression of gender inequity in Chile as violence. She emphasized that women face various forms of discrimination, including exploitation in drug trafficking, physical and emotional abuse, sexual assault, abandonment, humiliation, and degradation. She added that women suffer from direct violence, but also from institutional injustices within law enforcement. She recounted an incident involving university students who were detained following a demonstration, during which they were subjected to the degrading experience of being instructed to take off their clothes and then were sexually molested. Luisa reiterated, "Inequity is expressed very well in the situation of women, specifically in the various expressions of gender violence." Many women she sees who have suffered violence are addicted to drugs or alcohol. Luisa shared that women experience "emotional pain after being raped.

52 · CHAPTER 2

They begin to shrivel and become addicted to relieve their emotional pain." The types of violence that women experienced, from what Francisco witnessed in his work, included:

> Psychological, violent screaming, insults, humiliations, [and] physical . . . this year especially I've seen a lot of women . . . [who are] very depressed . . . because they have been beaten by their husband or partner. I don't know if it's more frequent than other parts of the country, but it's a very complex thing, yeah, here is very complex.

Marcela identified the physical impact on women's bodies who have suffered a lot of violence: "the position, for example, [in] your posture . . . there is some curvature of the back . . . inequity is something that has a physical effect on women." Violence permeated every aspect of a woman's experience, from a concrete physical experience to an experiential effect. Marcela described her friends as constantly talking about how tired they are: "How are you, my friend?" "Tired. How are you?" "Getting tired." She laughed, but the point is that women, especially in the impoverished sectors, embody the violence of inequity in bodily and concrete ways. Marcela reflected, "You never have time to be happy. If there is some space for freedom . . . it is always within the scope of the problem to solve for the day." Violence is normalized and women wear violence on their bodies, Marcela explained: "We're not beautiful, beauty is for women who do not experience everyday violence." She said, "another issue [of violence] for women is the societal expectation of what makes a woman credible." Further, Marcela added that women who live in poverty do not experience violence in the same way as other women:

> So when people tell me that violence is the same for every woman, I say "no," because for poor women it's much worse and it's much more complicated because they have a lot less support, real and concrete, because her body and her life are not hers.

Alma shared that the *Servicio Nacional de la Mujer* (SERNAM, National Women's Service) reported around 80 percent of women who live in Calama experienced various forms of violence. In the *consultorio* where Alma works, about half of the women they attend to have encountered some level of violence in their lives. This underscores the widespread and concerning issue of abuse that women in Calama face. She explained that physical and psychological violence is rampant, and pregnant women also suffer from physical and other forms of violence. The economy of Calama depends on mining, where a culture of *machismo* predominates. Alma stated, "Here it is very macho and still men beat women to feel more macho," emphasizing violence as a means to assert masculinity.

In this particular *consultorio* in the north of Chile, Alma noticed a marked social difference with adolescents. Girls at thirteen years old are pregnant, some of them the victims of sexual abuse, but others are in a consensual relationship with the goal of having children at thirteen or fourteen years old. Alma also knows of girls who are of a higher social class and want to study, but they end up having a baby, which destroys their plans. Other girls are in relationships with much older men, often twice their age, which puts them at high risk for various forms of control and violence.

I met Paloma in Santiago and spoke with her multiple times about the violent relationship she had with her husband. He was eleven years older than her, and their relationship began with him threatening to kill her father if she didn't marry him. At fourteen years old she had her first pregnancy. After that, he had affairs with women, sometimes in front of her in the home, and he would disappear for days on end and return with no explanation and no money. Paloma had to work to support her growing family, but this just made him jealous and more violent with her. While pregnant, she would sometimes wake to him pulling her outside by her hair. She suffered abuse in every way by her husband, including repeated sexual assault. With the help of a man, she was smuggled into Chile to search for work, leaving her children behind with her mom in Peru. It did not take much time for her husband to track her down in Chile, where the violence continued over many more years. She was in the process of separating from her husband during our first interview, but it was hard for her to stay away from her youngest, who remained with her husband. Paloma lived for her children and always put them first, frequently going without eating to make sure they had their basic needs met. From this marriage, she had four children and underwent four abortions, two of which took place in Chile.

While conducting fieldwork in the south of Chile, I met Mapuche women who were sexually abused within their families when they were young and physically abused in their marriage. Camila, a psychologist in a *consultorio* in the south of Chile, found that sexual and physical violence against Mapuche women was very high. Due to the rural environment that these women are in, they are not only isolated within their own communities, but also, to receive support for the abuse they are suffering, they would have to travel to another community that offered specific services, as many of the *consultorios* in rural areas are small and do not provide this type of focused support. However, Rayen explained that to work on violence within Mapuche communities, "you cannot only work with women, you have to work with men and with diverse genders as a collective."

54 · CHAPTER 2

This is part of the Mapuche worldview. Rayen told me, "to isolate violence, came from the outside." The contrast of what Camila is saying versus what Rayen is saying speaks to the differences between individualism and collectivism. How an issue is framed leads to subsequent interventions, which has the potential to perpetuate harm if a culturally responsive approach is not considered.

INSTITUTIONAL VIOLENCE

I heard multiple stories from women who had bad experiences within the public health care system. These ranged from not receiving relevant information to being denied services. While visiting a *población* on the north side of Santiago, I had a conversation with two women. One was an advisor for her sector in the community, and the other was an intermediary between the community and local *consultorio*. An intermediary is someone who listens to the issues or problems that people have with the *consultorio* and helps to advocate for changes. They told me the biggest complaint from the local community is how they are treated within the *consultorio*. Participants in this study echoed being treated poorly within the public health system across various geographic areas.

According to Marcela, who works at an NGO in the south of Chile, rural and Indigenous women were often treated badly within the public health system. It is the tone and the manner in which women are spoken to, for example: "But you have to do this, how do you not know how to do this?" In a tone of anger and frustration, Marcela asserted that certain women are questioned for not knowing and being treated as if they are stupid. "It is a violent treatment," she asserted. Emilia highlighted the issue of language barriers in the context of receiving quality care, especially for Indigenous women from neighboring countries. If someone does not understand what is being said, they are treated poorly. Even though the root of the issue is a language barrier, the solution is to blame the person who does not understand rather than to use an interpreter or explain it differently. Emilia reflected, "But it's not about understanding when a person speaks a different language."

Lack of information and choice within the public health system was also reflected in women's stories. After Emilia gave birth to her daughter, they put a Copper-T inside of her but never sought her consent. She was not given much information about it at all. The medical staff said, "Let's put this inside of you so you don't have any more problems." Emilia remembered that they never explained anything to her or told her how long she needed to have the Copper-T inside of her or when she should get a check-up. Emilia professed, "This only happens to poor women who do not have other resources." She explained that when you are poor, you do not have the right to exercise choice

Unpacking Inequity • 55

or decision-making, and you are not given the option to have information explained to you. According to Emilia, lack of information is a violent act and is connected to paternalistic treatment of women with limited resources, as control and morals are exerted over women within state institutions.

Esperanza had a miscarriage and was given misoprostol[2] to abort her fetus at home by herself. After she passed the fetus, she returned to the doctor to have the lining of her uterus scraped through a curettage procedure. She was worried about this procedure in case something went wrong and affected her ability to have children in the future. She said, "*No queria*" (I didn't want it). She directed all of her force and energy to rejecting this procedure. After the lining of her uterus was scraped, she found out the procedure was not necessary, because no tissue was found. Esperanza was upset because no one had explained that there was another option: "No one told me, 'let's wait and see what reaction your body has . . . if your body will eliminate the fetus by itself.' No one told me this." The only option given to Esperanza was misoprostol and curettage.

Discriminatory practices within public health spaces toward economically disadvantaged and Indigenous women create an unsafe environment and in turn a lack of trust in the public health system. Rayen shared that the reason why some Indigenous women do not go to the *consultorio* for a Pap test or to have their IUDs checked is because "they're treated bad. It's really tremendous that the people have to suffer in this way." Women who face economic challenges have historically experienced discrimination and exploitation within the public health system, with prejudicial attitudes being a major barrier to accessing quality reproductive health care. Maria José, who lives in a *campamento*, concurred, explaining that she does not like the way she is treated, so she never attempts to go to a *consultorio*.

Health professionals shared insights that highlighted the specific structural challenges that immigrant women face in the public health system. These women are confronted with national policies that restrict their mobility and access to resources. Alma, a *matrona* in a *consultorio* in the north of Chile, reported that immigrant women are discriminated against on all levels: "it's a pyramid and each [level] starts when they arrive in Chile undocumented." A large portion of immigrants living in the north of Chile live in Calama, home to the biggest open-pit copper mine in the world (Jarroud, 2015). The immigrant population in this region is mainly from Bolivia, Peru, Ecuador, and Colombia. While traveling in the area, I conducted one formal interview with a woman from Ecuador and five informal interviews with women from Bolivia, their ages ranging from early twenties to early thirties, and all but one traveled to Calama by themselves in search of work opportunities. In fact, they had all heard of Calama in their home country as a place where they could find employment. These women deal with many uncertainties. Young women who come to Calama by themselves and are unfamiliar with the area are at risk of abuse, economic exploitation, and forced prostitution.

Johanna, a young Bolivian woman I met, professed that she felt lucky because she found employment within four days with a good boss. She had heard stories of other women with bad experiences. She stated that sometimes bosses are not nice and there are a lot of women on the street in the sex work industry. Johanna traveled to Chile by herself, and she said that the journey was difficult, but she had a friend in Calama who greeted her, so she was not on her own, like many other women when they first arrive. Still, Johanna's situation was precarious. She entered Chile on a three-week tourist visa and she had already been in the country for two months. She wanted to return to Bolivia for a ten-day vacation to see her three children she left behind, but she was worried what might happen at the border, both in leaving Chile and in trying to enter again after violating the conditions of her visa.

Johanna's story is just one of many. Immigrant women face a plethora of issues: fear, depression, exploitation, abuse, loss of leaving their families and children behind, and lack of state support and protection. I visited a Catholic church where the sisters provided support to immigrant women through spiritual work, maternal support, listening, creating community, and providing resources and referrals. Sister Maria emphasized that undocumented women constantly face social and economic difficulties. These difficulties are the ramifications of structural violence, including poverty, racism, low levels of education, and lack of access to health and reproductive health services (Nuñez & Torres, 2007). Alma declared, "Those who are pregnant are actually discriminated against and undermined to the fullest. There is no law that will protect them." Further, Sister Maria stated that there is no prenatal care for undocumented women in this area, so these women just show up at the hospital when they are due to deliver, which affects both maternal and infant mortality rates. According to Nuñez and Torres (2007), in 2002 there were about 23,000 Peruvian women in Chile, of which over 75 percent were of reproductive age. These statistics show how large segments of the population are at risk of not receiving needed reproductive health services. Forty percent of births delivered at the hospital in Calama are immigrant women (Jarroud, 2015). Alma added, "In Antofogasta, the majority of stillbirths are born to foreign women" because they cannot access health care, "so these are very serious matters."

In theory, Chilean women with limited financial resources can access reproductive health care because there is some level of state protection. But participants highlight that this is not the case for immigrant women. Alma attributes this to both inherent inequities in society and lack of political will to allocate resources for immigrant women:

> There is discrimination and racism [and] there is a stereotype of the user population, especially women across the border. Then there is abuse, much, much abuse and because the system is, say, this system has no guidance to ensure the rights of the people. I think that [is] the underlying problem. It is a political decision that you want to keep the focus . . . on containing state spending.

Undocumented women in Chile face social and economic difficulties, not unlike other economically disadvantaged Chilean women discussed earlier. However, with the added component of immigrant status, multiple intersecting systems of oppression limit agency and choice. The difficulties for women who are marginalized in Chilean society are the result of everyday violence, such as poverty, racism, sexism, deficiency in education, and lack of access to health and reproductive health services (Nuñez & Torres, 2007).

According to Muñoz Cabrera (2010), age, "as a discriminatory mechanism, can intensify the social vulnerability of women who have multiple subordinated identities . . . age intersects with other dimensions of their identities in ways which intensify their isolation [and] exclusion" (p. 29). Some women discussed the judgment they received from others because they were sexually active adolescents. One young woman I spoke with went to a *consultorio* with her mother and was denied her right to access birth control because the *matrona* stated she was both too young and not currently in a committed relationship. Further, with the high rates of teen pregnancy (Estrada, 2009) and limited access to sexual education in schools (Casas & Ahumada, 2009), adolescent girls are targets of surveillance by multiple systems. These include families, public health care institutions, schools, and the church, contributing to further isolation when they face an unwanted pregnancy.

Conclusion

This chapter revealed how people have been relegated to the margins throughout Chilean history, signifying who has power in society and who does not. This dominant ideology or discourse is consistently recycled within the power dynamics of race, class, gender, and nation and is reinforced by key institutions, such as the government, the church, and public health institutions. An intersectional analysis helps to understand the multiple ways in which structural, cultural, and direct violence define women's experience of being criminalized for abortion in Chile. The various systems that influence women's lives—such as poverty, being Indigenous, lack of power, working as domestic laborers, being in abusive relationships, and living in a country with restrictive reproductive health policies—invites an exploration and understanding of the relationship between women, abortion, and criminalization. Framing abortion in a much broader context, such as historical and systemic violence and consequent barriers to health and economic resources, is integral in understanding women's lived experience when terminating a pregnancy.

CHAPTER 3

Centering Women

> Our bodies are not just biological entities; they are the territory through
> which we exist in the world, taking up skills and characteristics
> that, far from being innate, are socially and culturally constructed.
> —Maira, Hurtado, and Santana, 2010, p. 21

Centering women's voices in their own experience is critical as a social justice approach to knowledge production. It helps to inform what we know and understand about restrictive abortion policies and their impact on women. Constructing a framework that at its core, values the lived experience of women most harmed reveals the complexity of unequal power structures. Pía shared that "sometimes experiences are in our bodies and are not always in our words." Women who are sexually active and biologically capable have the potential to become pregnant. As Macarena, who had two abortions, expressed, "Every woman that is healthy has the possibility to get pregnant." However, the politics of abortion make it clear that abortion and the criminalization of women for abortion are framed along social and political, not biological, lines. Focusing on the body as a site of inquiry helps make intangible concepts of inequity tangible, highlighting the complex relationship between inequity and lived experience. This chapter highlights women's narratives of terminating their pregnancy within a highly criminalized environment, situating their voices and bodily experience as central to informing our knowledge base. The realities for women who had terminated a pregnancy demonstrate complex layers of inequity within clandestine spaces. This inequity is the result of structural violence and subsequent practices of exclusion, isolation, and erasure. Women's bodies also were marked by cultural discourse, further relegating women to the margins of society, which determined women's agency, sense of self, and displacement. In their abortion experience, women underscored the violence they endured, the fear surrounding

60 · CHAPTER 3

the illegality of abortion, the silence and invisibility that served as a constant reminder that they do not belong, the isolation and abandonment by the state, and the internalization of dominant discourses.

Violence

Women's agency is drastically reduced when they are compelled to put themselves in harmful situations. Within the clandestine nature of illegality, terminating a pregnancy generates devastating consequences, including life-threatening risks for women. Rafael, a documentary filmmaker who made a film about abortion in Chile, feels that "abortion is violent—the way society shames and treats women who have abortions, the way policies punish women, the way women hurt themselves, and the way women internalize this violence." Women who terminate their pregnancies embody many layers of violence. This violence was reflected in the lack of agency afforded to women concerning their abortion experience and the material impact of abortion on a woman's body within a clandestine environment.

Further, the illegality of abortion reinforces Chile's class structure. Illegality determines the abortion procedure's level of safety based on how much someone can pay. Ani shared that if you have financial resources, a woman may receive a safe and hygienic abortion in a secure clinic, even in an environment of criminality. However, for other women without funds, the abortion shifts to more high-risk methods. For the women who had little to no money, this determined how or whether they could terminate their pregnancy. For some women, lacking financial resources meant their only choice was to purchase herbs off the street, and these women did not always trust where they purchased the herbs or whether the herbs would work. In one of Paloma's abortion experiences, she had a strong adverse reaction from herbs she bought on the street, leading to significant pain without the intended outcome of terminating her pregnancy. For one of her abortions, Anaís went to a woman's house in an impoverished area outside of the city center, up in the hills. This woman told Anaís to drink many liters of water with *canela* (cinnamon) and to exercise heavily. Anaís was told "with a certain amount, you can drop the embryo, [but] this way of abortion did not give me results." Anaís was in search of a different way to have an abortion, and she found a woman she thought worked as a street performer, "*que bailada en la calle*" (who danced in the street). Receiving an abortion from the street performer was dangerous for Anaís because the woman had no knowledge of health. I asked Anaís why she enlisted the help of the street performer, and she replied that it was because she did not have any money, "*nada, nada,*

nada" (nothing, nothing, nothing). This was the cheapest route for her. Often these experiences happen inside of marginalized spaces that are "very poor, very dirty," Anaís reflected.

Some women with limited resources terminated their pregnancy through a medical procedure, but not necessarily with a medical professional. These women made do with who was available, rather than being able to look for the best care. Women often terminated their pregnancies in unsanitary environments because they had no choice. Constanza had one of her abortions at a house where the woman who performed the abortion lived. Constanza remembers that the abortion was performed on a bed "where someone slept, they just put a sheet [on the bed] and did the abortions there." The clandestine condition created by restrictive policies put economically disadvantaged women's health and lives at risk, without eliminating abortions.

Contrary to this experience, Pía, who had access to financial resources, and Anaís, who borrowed money for two of her abortions to allow her access to a safer abortion, were able to go to medical professionals to terminate their pregnancies. This is a common practice among women of middle to upper class. Although having access to financial resources can enhance personal agency, it did not necessarily ensure a sanitary environment or good treatment from the abortion provider. For example, Pía gave an example of one location that she visited. It was an old house with many women sitting in one room waiting for an abortion. "There were six or seven cats moving around these women," and this made her feel uncomfortable, so she left. Pía had a measure of choice not afforded to women without resources. Pía went to multiple places before choosing a location that she trusted to terminate her pregnancy. The woman who performed Pía's abortion was polite, and Pía had confidence in her medical knowledge, but the context of illegality during the 1970s did nothing to ensure a healthy environment. Pía remembered:

> Well, this was a house, a very normal house [with] a garden . . . I went to the second floor and what I remember is . . . the light bulb. This was a room with a bed, nothing else, it was a very common room, nothing about sanitary conditions, nothing that you could recognize that this was a room for abortions. This also means that it was insecure, I imagine, because it was like any room, no sanitization, nothing like that.

Anaís, who terminated two of her pregnancies in the late 1990s at a medical clinic with a private physician, did not have any fear regarding her health, and the clinic was a hygienic environment, but she said the doctor had a sinister face. She heard a rumor that this doctor was from the time of the dictatorship,

62 · CHAPTER 3

so she did not feel comfortable with him. She felt this doctor was distant, as if he had no intention of caring for his patient. Thus, clandestine spaces often fostered distrust and hostility, even within a medical environment.

Despite the negative aspects of Anaís's and Pía's experiences, women who have more resources generally have some level of protection, even in an illegal context. Having social and economic resources and being able to trust in the provider greatly influenced women's perception of how they felt about themselves when terminating a pregnancy. Marcela's friend who had access to financial resources left Chile to terminate her pregnancy in a country where abortion was legal. Her friend was safe, no one questioned her, and so she did not question herself. She had a sense of self-worth, Marcela reflected.

Macarena, who had two abortions, experienced something similar. Her second abortion took place in Mexico, where under certain circumstances she could terminate her pregnancy legally. She felt supported by the gynecologist, who told her and her partner, "The most important thing is that you two are secure, are safe, and are sure about your decision." It was empowering for Macarena to have support and information, and it made her feel like "We are doing something good, you know, in a good way." This emphasizes the distinct experience of having a supportive context versus the environment of inequity and illegality, which is disempowering and puts women's health and lives at risk. Ani reflected: "having the backing of legality makes a big difference for women, because at least they have this right versus having no right at all . . . having no rights creates a highly vulnerable situation and experience for women." Pía conveyed her thoughts of the lived experience of inequity around abortion for women during the dictatorship:

> Of course I recognize my experience is the experience of middle class that [gave me] the possibility of doing it in the best conditions. I think that [class] differences make a big difference among women. I remember, for example, listening to women that did [an abortion] with the *sonda* technique[1] . . . they went with this hose [inside of them] two or three days. I just cannot think of equality, it's impossible to believe in equality because I remember one of them was telling me the story, I was almost going to faint listening to her. . . . That makes the experience of being a woman really different. I have not had to go to work with something in my body . . . imagine when you do it in such aggressive conditions with your body and also with all this clandestine thing around it.

Many participants highlighted that the act of abortion was violence to their bodies. Paz shared that the only way to terminate a pregnancy was through an intervention and that intervention is violent to your body. She used misoprostol to terminate her pregnancy, which is a relatively safe procedure if used correctly. However, Paz reflected that there is an economy generated around putting chemicals in your body, and in this sense, there is no ritual or meaning attached to the process. She stated that "you have to search, you have to pay, [and] you have to risk. You have to take pills and put pills inside of your body and it's not natural." Paz was in a lot of pain. She shared that it felt as if someone had their hand inside of her uterus and was squeezing, twisting, and turning her insides, "to stop being pregnant, it's intense."

For other women who terminated their pregnancies with the *sonda* technique, they expressed experiencing a lot of pain in their body, both from the actual technique and for Anaís, the infection that developed afterward. Anaís used the *sonda* technique for the two abortions she had in a *población*. The second time, she experienced a lot of physical pain and remembers it was more complicated due to getting an infection from the procedure. The infection was not bad enough to warrant a hospital visit, for which Anaís was grateful, "but it's very dangerous because of the infections." The *sonda* was a dangerous method of terminating a pregnancy and was used only on economically disadvantaged women who had no other resources. Constanza remembered, "The *sonda*, the most dangerous in this country. It was only used on poor women, it was something very common [for poor women]." Pilar was a teenager when she terminated her pregnancy. She recalled being extremely bloated and that she could not help but scream because the *sonda* was incredibly painful, stating, "It was not just my body that was hurting, but also my spirit." She was crying as she relived the pain and sadness of this experience. Marcela witnessed the dangerous nature of this procedure for her friend, and its inherent violence and the lack of safer alternatives left her with a sense of powerlessness. She recollected that watching her friend go through this was painful for her as well. She is not against abortion and believes women should have the autonomy to make their own decision, but she reiterated that it is better for the health and well-being of women if abortion can be a less physically and emotionally traumatizing experience. No woman shared that abortion was easy or that it was something they wanted to do to their body. Being compelled into high-risk situations that posed a threat to their lives highlights the inequity of the illegality of abortion and its disproportionate impact on women. The physical harm women endured underscored the tangible and undeniable nature of violence, transforming the abstract into a concrete reality within their bodies.

Facing the Unknown

Women shared experiencing varying levels of fear surrounding their abortion experiences: fear of being sexual, of violence, of the unknown, for their bodies and their lives, of the law, and of others finding out, both that they were pregnant and that they had an abortion. The body was a site of enduring fear.

64 · CHAPTER 3

Esperanza pointed out that in Chilean society, there is little discussion about "sexuality, reproduction, and menstruation." She was thankful that she was able to learn many things from her mother, but these teachings were continually fraught with fear, in part because her mother "suffered greatly in childbirth. Obviously she had fear and all of this she passed on to me." Esperanza had "fear of the first sexual relationship, fear of getting sexuality transmitted infections, fear of childbirth, [and] fear of abortion. Fear of everything!" Her sexuality began with embodying fear. This bodily experience of holding on to fear for Esperanza was transferred to her from her mother. In contrast, Macarena has never lived with so much fear as she does now that she has a daughter. She reflected, "So, all of my fears will transfer to her. All of the things that she will live, I will live, and all that happens to her, will happen to me. If she is raped, it will be like I was raped." These examples of transference between mother and daughter for both Esperanza and Macarena demonstrate how fear is a bodily experience, capable of being passed on from one body to another. Their stories also reveal the potential vulnerability of women's bodies. The fear produced from clandestine environments has an equal opportunity to be passed on to women who seek abortions in these spaces.

Being forced to navigate clandestine spaces was a new and difficult experience for women. Entering into an unfamiliar area to get an abortion produced fear. These women had to visit neighborhoods they were not familiar with and go to a stranger's house. Anaís talked about a *población* in a rural area that she had never been to before, although the man with whom she was pregnant was from this community. Before going to the *población*, she was told to be careful entering the community and the particular house because the woman who was the abortion provider lived there with her family. She said, "It was not like entering an office." An office is a neutral space, and a home is an intimate space. The clandestine nature of the situation, combined with feeling exposed, produced fear for her.

Paz was apprehensive about acquiring misoprostol online. This was an illegal act. She expressed concern about the consequences of the clandestine nature of illegality and the challenges she faced in navigating it. Paz and her partner searched the internet to find people who sold misoprostol. She expressed discomfort with this, explaining that it felt impersonal, since they had to buy from an unknown person whose primary motive was monetary gain, not her health and well-being. She noted the obvious risks associated with putting the pills inside her body and shared that she was really afraid to do this, not knowing if what she bought was truly misoprostol or some other drug that was harmful to her. But she did not have the financial resources for a safe abortion experience.

Centering Women • **65**

Although the clandestine spaces that women navigated were distinct from one another, women revealed a similar experience of fear surrounding the underground nature of their abortion, and for some, an element of hostility in their experience.

Women also expressed fear of not being in control, because they did not have access to information and they were afraid to ask questions. For example, Macarena, a teenager at the time, went to a house in a *población* that made her feel insecure because she was unfamiliar with the area. A woman opened the door and offered her and her boyfriend a seat. They waited for forty-five minutes and she remembered seeing a woman who came out of a room, looking tired, and as if she was crying. Macarena thought, "Oh my god, maybe there is a lot of pain." She was trying to build a story in her head of what was going to happen, trying to understand, because she was afraid to ask any questions.

> If I ask any questions and they feel insecure, maybe they say, "We don't want to [do anything] with you, leave from here." I don't want to do that because I need to do the abortion. . . . [Also] I start to talk with my boyfriend and I say, "I need to ask them what they're [going] to do with me," and he [answered], "no, you can't ask any question[s], you will enter and ask nothing, don't ask nothing."

Macarena was also fearful for her health:

> I was scared . . . [to] have other problems because one of the things is sometimes you go to get an abortion and something went wrong and then you get sick and then you need to go to [the] hospital . . . so, that is like the worst thing that you can live, you know, like I want to have an abortion, but I don't want the abortion [to] put me in a worse situation, and so I was [worried] about all these things.

Not knowing what was going to happen to their bodies produced uncertainty for women. Paz remembered:

> I was worrying about my health, but I was sure that I want to do it, so I make the decision and I do it. I take the first pill and I know that I started . . . I remember that I was clear that I want to do that, but also I have like a confusion . . . inside . . . the fear was more [about] the pills, the way to do it. I had doubt about my health. It's weird because you know it's going to be a lot of blood and maybe you can pass out . . . you don't know the real thing until you do it. So, I was insecure about that.

Multiple women expressed fear of dying due to an abortion complication. Paloma knew a woman who had died from an abortion. With the first abortion she had at seventeen years old, she had a lot of fear about losing her life and leaving her two children behind. Pilar expressed a similar fear. Her friends told her she would bleed a lot and could die. And Macarena had heard of women who had died:

> I was scared because I had heard about many cases of women that [died] in the moment [during] the abortion or after the abortion . . . or they felt bad, or something was wrong, or they put something inside you that made you feel bad and then you're dead . . . and always I was thinking if the doctor was a real doctor or just any woman.

Women also voiced concern about the potential legal consequences resulting from health complications. It was scary for women to think of having to seek treatment at a public hospital if any health issues arose from terminating their pregnancy in illegal circumstances. As one woman shared, "if you were hemorrhaging, it was a risk." Women who terminated their pregnancy with the *sonda* method were especially fearful of complications arising, as it was a dangerous technique that might necessitate emergency care. Also, the *sonda* was more easily detectable compared to a more modern method, such as misoprostol. If women went to a public hospital, they were at risk of coming into contact with law enforcement, further exacerbating their fears. Macarena recollected that if you arrived at the hospital with complications from an illegal abortion, the *Carabiñeros* would be called and you could get into legal trouble.

Women also voiced concern about the possibility of others discovering their pregnancy and subsequent abortion. Macarena shared:

> [I was] afraid because I don't want to be pregnant and I started to feel very bad, like vomiting . . . physically bad, and so it was a very hard time because I don't want my mom [to] realize that I am pregnant. I was completely afraid because . . . we need to hide that I am pregnant, and I feel bad and nervous, with a lot of fear.

Paloma struggled with two distinct issues, the fear of fatal consequences from having an abortion and the fear of disclosing this particular pregnancy to her husband. Because of her husband's jealousy, she was afraid that sharing the news of her pregnancy would lead him to accuse her of cheating and become abusive. Paloma was adamant that she had never been with anyone besides her husband, "*ni uno*" (not one), but she was afraid to have an abortion and afraid of her husband's reaction if he found out she was pregnant. There was no space for her to be in her own experience.

Many women interviewed disclosed they had not talked about their abortion experience in a long time, if ever. Pilar told me that she had kept her abortion story to herself and was not sure what her daughters, both teenagers then, would think of her if they knew. Women held profound fear in their bodies on multiple levels, and holding on to the fear around their abortion experience was a profound, deep-kept secret. The social, economic, and political context of abortion creates the condition where women do not have a voice in their own experience.

Invisibility and Silence

The emphasis on criminalization creates a situation where women had no agency or active role in shaping their abortion experience. When sharing their stories, women were often reliving the silence they had held on to for many years due to the clandestine nature of the illegal context. Women's voices were suppressed and constrained, the stories buried deep within them, sometimes for years. Without a place to voice what they remember of their experience, the consequence is that their experience is defined for them by state policies and cultural discourse on abortion.

For many women, having an abortion is a deep secret they had not shared with anyone. Anaís did not tell anyone, "*no lo conté nadie*" (I told no one), about two of the four abortions that she had. In part this was because these pregnancies were the product of "only sex," and not from being in a relationship. During the interview it was also difficult for Anaís to reveal that she had four abortions. She seemed hesitant to share, as if she was awaiting my response before opening up to me about the next abortion. I had no judgment toward her one way or the other, and in time she was more comfortable to open up about the other experiences, and she eventually told me that she felt shame about having had four abortions. I received a similar response from Paloma, who also had four abortions. She was concerned about what my reaction would be. This demonstrated how deep the secrecy and shame are that women are holding on to in their bodies.

Macarena felt the context of criminalization makes abortion taboo. She explained, "You can't talk about it with everybody. Like if you say, 'I had an abortion, or two abortions, or three abortions,' you are a bad person, you have problems. You are a murderer." In the *población* where Pilar was from, women who aborted in the late 1980s and early 1990s did not talk about their abortion experience with anyone. She said that there are many issues in the community, like abortion, that no one ever talked about because it was "very taboo, very secret and hidden." She continued, "You have to keep it very quiet, or you will get judgments from others." Pilar's mother was very critical of her, and her boyfriend at the time put all the blame on her. In this way, women do not exist

68 · CHAPTER 3

in their experience, but rather through the discourse that others project onto them.

Marisol, whose family fled Chile during the dictatorship, had an abortion in the host country within a semi-legal context. She discussed the context of her decision not to share with her family that she had an abortion.

> [My family had a] Catholic upbringing and I don't know whether it was really Catholic, but moral, where sexuality was at the central core of it and how women should behave in order to get respect from the men around them. So . . . when my abortion did take place and my mom continued to have basically the same . . . I never told her. . . . [also] they always placed quite a lot of expectations, too many, far too many expectations of my performance, my accomplishments. It's like for them, I was going to be what they never were. My mom didn't even finish elementary education, my father did not even finish high school education. They came, both of them, [from] very poor, working-class backgrounds . . . I knew that if they found out that I had gotten pregnant, it was a let down . . . so, I think it would have been really, really, really difficult for them to deal with it. And even up to that point my mom never talked about birth control, never talked about sexuality, it's like what are you going to tell them, "eh mom I got pregnant, eh mom, I got an abortion."

Families' expectations presented an issue for other women as well. For example, Pilar's mom had plans for her. Her mother dreamed that her daughter would get out of the *población*. However, living in a community with limited economic opportunities, Pilar questioned, where was she going to get exposure to something else? Women kept silent about their pregnancies and abortion experiences, in part because they would not be able to live up to family expectations.

For Paloma and Pilar, the silence was literally embodied through swallowing physical pain. For one of Paloma's abortions, she went to a doctor. This doctor told her to be quiet when she was experiencing a lot of pain and threatened to kick her out of his office if she made any sounds. Pilar, an adolescent when she had her abortion through the *sonda* technique, cried out in pain from the intensity of the contractions she was feeling. Her mother told her to be quiet or the neighbors would hear. Paloma and Pilar silenced their very concrete bodily pain, reflecting that they did not have space in their experience.

The silence surrounding women's experiences with abortion extended to medical professionals as well, which makes it difficult to accurately assess the prevalence of abortion and to provide needed services. Alma pointed out that due to the illegality of abortion, a basic understanding of abortion is lacking in Calama because women do not talk about it. As a psychologist, Francisco emphasized his focus on providing emotional support rather than dwelling on the legal repercussions. However, he noted that he cannot say the same for his colleagues, because they do not talk about abortion. When they do learn about abortion cases, there tends to be a sense of discomfort, leading women to withdraw from seeking supportive services. The silence surrounding abortion is so pervasive that health care professionals often become aware of it only when complications arise and a woman goes to the emergency room, making the invisible visible only in the context of health complications and legal circumstances, further perpetuating the stigma around abortion.

During interviews, women clearly articulated what they needed, emphasizing the importance of being supported by female health professionals. However, an environment of illegality creates the condition where women cannot ask for what they need. Women felt invisible, as if they were not "existing in the experience," as Pía reflected. Behnke (2003) suggests that a "body breaks the silence and announces itself to us when something goes wrong and our own body presents itself to us as an object" (p. 7). When an experience is objective versus subjective, "we do not experience in our experiencing" (p. 7). Thus, women's bodies are moving within these clandestine spaces, and there is silence there, because these spaces do not exist. Pía shared:

> I realized what to be a woman meant, this idea of clandestinity about a situation that so often happens in women's lives, all this secret because you have the experience . . . it's something with my identity that has a sort of footprint that's there and it opens you to leave or to inhabit your body in a different way. But what's hard, I think, is that something happens to you . . . [that] cannot exist. I would say that was the most . . . violent, but it's a hidden violence that takes out some sort of trusting in society or that I have a place here.

Pía was involved in clandestine political work after the coup d'état, but the clandestine nature of abortion was more profound for her than her underground political work.

> [It] was really out of my imagination and any similar experience. I remember going to two or three places before with this secret [to have an abortion] that makes you become . . . immediately you become different. You're moving through places that do not exist. And I remember thinking that the political clandestine work was nothing [in comparison]. Because certainly you could be surprised and you could go to jail, but here [with abortion] it was your body, it took place in your body and also all this silence about that.

Many women felt violated by not having a voice or a place to "exist" in their own experience. The biggest violation for Esperanza was "the little capacity she had to decide." And for Macarena, the most serious issue was that she did

70 · CHAPTER 3

not have any choice. In this way, silence or the inability to choose represented state violence against women.

Paz explained what having little space to choose in a repressive environment was like for her:

> You're trying not to hurt anyone, but you feel like shit always because you have to do things in the darkness . . . and also you have a lot of questions, you don't have a face to make those questions [to], like a person that you go and you say, "I have this question, I feel this way," it doesn't exist, it is all virtual . . . [the state] is making you feel like shit . . . why are they appearing in my abortion? Why am I thinking about that when I am in the pain of something personal? I feel rage in that moment because they are in all the places in our lives, where is the freedom?

Participants discussed poor women as not able to make decisions freely about their bodies, that their body is not their own. When I asked Emilia who has control over their bodies, she responded by saying, "the state, because the state determines who gets health care and if a woman needs to seek a clandestine abortion." Moving within clandestine spaces without an ability to voice their experience created invisibility, and consequently, women did not exist in the experience.

Isolation

All the women interviewed about their abortion experience mentioned distinct forms of isolation. Women discussed the consequences of sharing their pregnancy with others, of being alone in their pregnancy and abortion experience, of feeling alone, even when they were with others, and of being abandoned by the state without any protection or access to information or professional support.

Constanza was with a man who was part of the liberation theology movement, which helped to unearth her political identity as a Mapuche activist, so she was very taken by him. However, this man was already married and had a child, and he left Constanza as soon as he found out she was pregnant. Thus, she was on her own. Constanza went to a *población* to receive her abortion. She brought her son with her because she did not have anyone to watch him for her. She also had a friend accompany her to get the abortion, but this friend could not escort her home. After the abortion, Constanza felt weak, but she made the long trek home across Santiago by bus with her baby in her arms. She described feeling something deep inside of her when she was on the bus. It was not guilt or loss, because she knew that she was not ready to have another child. However, in this moment she had a profound realization that she was completely alone, sitting on a bus with her son in her arms, in silence. Constanza felt rage toward the man she became pregnant with. She revealed a big disconnect between her head and what she knew was happening, and her heart, including the loss of the companionship that she longed for. The pain she felt in her body was sadness, the sadness of being alone in this experience.

Pilar became pregnant the first time she had sex as a teenager, and both her mother and her boyfriend at the time expressed anger with her. Her mother called her a whore and her boyfriend called her a murderer. She felt abandoned by the two people closest to her. Pilar did have a positive experience with the abortion provider: "She was very caring to women, not like *una bruja* [a witch], but full of love, a very good person." However, when the community in the *población* found out that this woman provided abortions, the provider had to leave the community. This was especially sad for Pilar, as the one person who supported her when she felt abandoned was ostracized from the community, leaving Pilar feeling more alone than before. Pilar suffered from depression for many years because of the isolation she felt in her abortion experience. When I asked Pilar how she felt talking about her experience in the interview, she disclosed feelings of loneliness. However, after sharing what she went through, she felt a little lighter and less alone. Other women discussed similar sentiments regarding feeling less alone after sharing, validating the importance of women having a safe and trusting place to voice and normalize their experience, decreasing their sense of isolation.

Esperanza described using misoprostol, which she received from a public health institution, to terminate her nonviable pregnancy. She was at home alone when she inserted the pills inside of her vagina, despite the recommendations from international organizations that advocate for misoprostol use to avoid being alone in case of potential complications (Women on Waves, n.d.). She went through the abortion process by herself, but it was not her choice to be alone. It was difficult for Esperanza not to have anyone with her or to be able to ask for any support. She cried during the interview, reliving the sadness of being alone in her abortion experience with this tragic loss of losing her child. After aborting her fetus, she was not offered any resources through public health. She felt ignorant and no information was given to her. Further, with abortion, it is secret, so hardly anyone knows. But with a miscarriage, also known as a spontaneous abortion, it is difficult to have space to feel the loss. Esperanza was often asked, "When are you going to get pregnant again?" Thus, she did not feel she had a voice in her own experience, and this made her feel alone.

However, even for Macarena and Paz, who had their partners with them before, during, and after the abortion, they still felt alone. This was explained as not feeling that their partners, who were with them during the abortion, had the tools or the experience to support them. In part, this was due to their partners being young, like them, with no experience of their own. Macarena reflected:

> The reality is that I didn't know what to do or how to channel my feelings, so . . . I was always waiting for my boyfriend to transmit to me security and to feel safe, but he can't because he was the same, a young guy and inexperienced. So, I was waiting for something . . . that never came. That made me feel frustrated and he was the only person next to me and so in that point, I felt alone, "if you can't give me anything that I need, I'm alone" . . . that was hard. I remember having the deep feeling that we are alone in this world. We are alone, it's your decision and nobody will understand why you make this decision. Nobody will understand what is going on inside of you, in your mind, in your life, in your feelings, so you are alone and that kind of decision is [a] very, very deep decision.

Paz remembered:

> I was with my partner and I felt the need to be alone. So, I went to the bathroom and I closed the door and I sit in the bathroom and I start to feel really painful, like sensations inside my body and I remember that I was thinking a lot of things. In a moment I had to put my head on the floor because I was feeling like I'm going to pass out and I was really thinking that it was humiliating. Why do we have to do things like this, for girls, with no one to take care of you, like an experienced person? It was feeling not normal . . . I really need a woman, like an old woman to tell me it's going to be ok . . . but I also didn't want to be with my partner because he was preoccupied, "are you ok, are you ok," so, I can't tell him that I'm ok, because I was really not that fine. But I know it's going to be fine, but I can't explain that to him with the pain. I really miss a woman, like, an experienced woman.

Because of the illegality of abortion, women were relegated to negotiate clandestine spaces and experiences on their own. Several women in this study expressed feeling alone and abandoned by the state. Paz described what it was like for her to purchase misoprostol online through the black market:

> They can lie to you and you are vulnerable. You have to trust in a virtual world. You don't have a face to anyone, it's all on the phone [and] on the internet. It's very strange because in one moment you are totally alone because no one is anyone.

Paz had a lot of sadness and pain around her experience. She expressed disappointment in not being able to coordinate and get help, and that there was no professional to answer her questions. She stated, "Where are the women? The structure doesn't allow for this."

Pilar voiced that "with abortion, you are very alone, you can't go see a psychologist or choose where you want to go to have the abortion." Reproductive health policies that treat all women as if they are the same fail to take into account each woman's situation. Many influences make women feel extremely vulnerable. Each woman's situation is distinct and personal. Paz expressed feeling as if "you are like a number in that moment. You have to trust when someone tells you something . . . but it might not be the right thing." Thus, women expressed feeling vulnerable to abuse and exploitation because of lack of state abortion regulation and protection.

Francisco conveyed the problem as women not getting support if they want or need it:

> It's a big problem because we know that [women] are doing it [abortion], but they don't get help for it and some die. For example . . . there is a case about a woman who had an abortion, there is a lot of bleeding, she can die so she goes to the emergency room. Everybody finds out and then it gets to the local authorities [then] you have the police there in the hospital and she is condemned.

An illegal context creates a lack of ethical professional response, which further isolates women. Luisa stated that health professionals do not usually ask if women have had an abortion. Instead they ask, "How many pregnancies? How many children?" Luisa explained:

> It is not in the care of legitimate health, there is no legitimacy for the experience of abortion from the professional, the health professional. Then women go on the defensive and they are careful what they say because in the end [women can be] legally sanctioned . . . so, women are limited to share . . . there [are] few spaces, very few spaces [women] have to process collectively and to have the confidence to speak. . . . There's a very big punishment in society and in the subjectivity of women.

Marcela has accompanied many women in their abortions because women suffer, have a lot pain, and are alone in their abortion experience. Marcela explained that the women she has accompanied could not ask questions of or tell their families, partners, or friends about their abortion. She thinks this is what hurts women the most, being isolated, more than the actual risks of abortion. She continued by saying that women who abort are discriminated against, violated, and rejected "because people here have a different perspective. Most think [abortion] is murder." Sutton (2010) explains that the illegality of abortion reinforces structural inequities and keeps abortion clandestine in the physical environment, as well as a woman's internal embodied environment.

Internalized Oppression

Several women shared their experiences of internalizing the narratives that surround their pregnancies and abortions. Abortion, for them, involves not just defying the legal system but also challenging deeply ingrained cultural and societal norms. Laws have been shown not to protect women, but rather to foster a discriminatory environment that gives others permission to treat women poorly in health and in the eye of the law. Economically disadvantaged women, especially, must struggle against multiple layers of discrimination in society, which transfers to their abortion experience. Women discussed feeling responsible for their actions and behaviors. This caused them to internalize blame and negative messages, in addition to embodying emotions of sadness, anger, and rage. The latter resulted in some women critiquing the structure of social norms, moving toward a process of finding peace and strength.

Because of the cultural responsibility placed on women, women interviewed described blaming themselves for being pregnant, having an abortion, and for having an unviable fetus. Anaís explained that the most difficult for her regarding her abortion was her self-recrimination for not being responsible: "I felt very violated with the abortion, in myself." The context of illegality created a violent condition in which her abortions took place. Anaís felt violated but also responsible. She experienced contradictory emotions. When I asked where she developed the idea that she was responsible, she explained, "When you talk about sexuality, when you talk about kids, or your capacity to reproduce, [the state] always speaks of the *exigencia* [requirement] that the woman has to take responsibility." As she struggled to explain further, Anaís said, for example, women are supposed to be controlling their reproduction with pills, but women are not always driving the situation. Many things are going on at the same time, whether you are interested in the pleasure aspect, or you do not want to bother the other person, or you do not have the energy to make a decision, or there is intimidation because the other is demanding. Many questions intervene in the moment that make one vulnerable. So it is not just a question of sexuality being "automatic or mechanical." Anaís said that if you have prevention information and you know how to use birth control, then you have no excuse, none whatsoever "to fail." However, she continued, it is not mechanical or automatic, because so many other things influence that situation in the moment. For example, "What is your identity, your relationship to others? And as a woman, what is your relationship to your body? Are you the owner of your own body to make your decisions? It's very complex."

Anaís highlighted multiple facets of the societal context that contribute to women internalizing blame, particularly feeling responsible for becoming pregnant. This internalization can be disempowering and give rise to inner conflicts in women. Paz, on the other hand, expressed her discomfort when obtaining misoprostol from the black market. She struggled with feelings of shame, as if she were engaging in criminal activity from buying misoprostol illegally. She shared that it is strange to be handed pills in a Ziploc bag:

> It's weird because there are pills . . . in a Ziploc bag, it's like you're feeling like you're doing something bad . . . always in your head the thing you are doing is not only emotional, but also a legal thing, you know, you are lying to the government. So that feels weird because you feel bad.

Paz voiced that she is a good person, but she had to go through with her decision to have an abortion. For Paz, the clandestine nature of abortion "contaminates the process, the feeling of the process," resulting in a disconnection between herself and her body.

Marcela explained that women who have abortions carry a lot of guilt that is instilled in them from others, but the guilt and shame "is not theirs." Macarena agreed: "They are ideas, prejudices, constructed by culture." She continued to share that the most troubling aspect of the concept of abortion is the notion that it involves taking someone's life, equating it to the act of murder. The word "kill" carries profound moral and emotional weight: "I never killed anyone, I killed an ant, you know?" The assertion that abortion equates to taking a life is deeply unsettling, as no woman shared that she wanted to take another person's life: "I'm not killing a baby. I don't want to kill anybody." A friend of Macarena's had an abortion, and she told Macarena, "I am a bad person, I am breaking all my education . . . I cannot forgive myself." The education she was ⸢erring to was from the church. Macarena's friend came from an especially reli̖̖gious family,

> I tried to explain [to] her how normal this is, how necessary . . . and it's not her fault. The idea to be guilty . . . comes from the Catholic moral, you know, because there is a difference to feel responsible and to be *culpable*, you know, to be *culpable* is a moral idea . . . [and] when you are *culpable*, you carry things that are not yours. and then I realize that the traumatized situation comes from the context, not from the abortion.

The political and cultural discourse, rather than the actual situation of abortion, creates the condition where women embody feelings of guilt and shame.

76 · CHAPTER 3

For Paz, the clandestine nature of abortion and having to navigate within the black-market economy brought up feelings of rage:

> It's not a game, it's not funny, it's not a rite, it's not healthy, and it's not natural . . . why do you have to do things in this way? Another way to do it would be in a loving way, but you have to do it with all that shit. . . . The most profound emotions in our life are mediated [by] the economy . . . you know in your heart it is not normal, but it's [also] not moral [and] it's not religious, it's another thing. It's weird.

In contrast to the passive acceptance of embodying the political and cultural discourse on sexuality and abortion, Paz reflected on what is important for women to think about:

> The first thing [to ask] is how you feel about yourself and how do you feel about yourself with a partner, or someone you are having sex with. Do you want to be there or not . . . Do you want to be penetrated . . . do you want to be pregnant, do you not want to be pregnant, are you having caring sex, are you having violent sex? I don't know, the first thing to think is about that. Are you conscious that you are having the possibility [to get pregnant] when you are in that act because it's a possibility? It's always a possibility, with condoms, without condoms, with pills, without pills, it's always a possibility [to get pregnant]. So the family, the people who surround that couple, or person, [are] they willing to listen, support, or [do they] punish, treat them badly? After, how do you feel? Do you feel bad, do you want to talk, do you want to have a child, do you not want to have a child?

Similar to what Anaís shared, there are many layers that determine a woman's experience. Paz expressed that women need to ask these questions for themselves and not listen to the limitations that the political and cultural discourse determine for women. She continued:

> Are we doing it in a way that we want to do things or do we want others to make decisions for us? Perfect bodies, perfect sex, what does it mean? In that moment are you there? Not them. And the moment of abortion is the same question, are you there, is your mother there, or your grandmother is there telling you that you don't have to do it, or is it your position, your economic [position] . . . what is the context in our lives that we are making the decision like that? And the publicity on the TV, the abortion is really bad, like, it's not for Christian people . . . it's like for weird people, for lesbians, for young people, but everyone does it. It's all a lie and we have to unify ourselves and realize that we have things in common . . . we are not that lost if we have things in common.

Women's internalized feelings of shame demonstrated cultural violence aimed specifically toward women because it is the context of cultural discourse around abortion that creates these feelings. In a different context, these feelings would not exist. The construction of abortion is multifaceted in that women embody multiple levels of inequity simultaneously. Women who have terminated their pregnancies go against gender and cultural expectations and against the law. The embodied reality around abortion keeps women isolated and separate from each other. Although many women have experience with abortion, in the context of illegality, abortion is a deeply held secret, which subsequently deprives women of their identity, experience, and voice.

Conclusion

This chapter revealed women's experience with abortion within the context of illegality and clandestine spaces. Women from various backgrounds experience many of the same issues within a legal or illegal context. These include having to navigate family dynamics and expectations, relationships, and economic circumstances. However, the legal context makes a big difference for women by affording women rights. The illegal context of abortion takes away any rights that women should have, making them vulnerable to abuse, exploitation, and other forms of systemic and personal harm. I was continually struck by the generosity and courage of the women who shared their abortion stories with me in a context of illegality. In a society that does not give women space to have a voice, women speaking out challenged the silence that had been imposed on them.

The condition of illegality fosters a clandestine environment that leads to the emergence and perpetuation of an underground economy related to abortion. This, in turn, exacerbates women's vulnerability and exploitation, particularly when the state fails to provide necessary safeguards. More specifically, for economically disadvantaged women, the underground economy severely restricts their agency and decision-making power, as they often cannot afford to buy "choice." Consequently, these women find themselves in perilous situations, as the absence of state protection in the black market exposes them to harm. In this context, women are marginalized, as violence, fear, silence, and isolation become interwoven into their lives, leaving indelible marks on their physical and emotional bodies. When abortion is reduced to a crime, by which a woman is measured, she is stripped of her identity and the context that her decision was made in. She is subsequently held responsible for the ills of society and labeled and treated as *other*.

78 · CHAPTER 3

Just as women's identities and abortion experiences are defined by multiple interlocking systems of oppression, such as race, class, and gender, so is the potential for contestation within these systems of oppression. Despite many barriers negotiating and embodying the inequity in cultural discourse and clandestine spaces, women revealed a resistance. Thus, the body is a site of inequity and resistance simultaneously, across time and social location (Caputo, 2010). No matter the risk in the face of inequity, repression, or marginalization, women's capacity to resist was constant.

CHAPTER 4

¡Resistencia!

> Political resistance involves, first and foremost, putting the
> material body in action to affect the course of society. . . .
> Wounded bodies, tortured bodies, defiant bodies, bodies that
> confront repression, bodies that protest in surprising ways,
> and out-of-place bodies shape both the political landscape
> and the embodied consciousness of participants.
>
> —Sutton, 2010, p. 161

Throughout Chilean history, there has been a visible culture of resistance. The Indigenous peoples of Chile have struggled against the Incas, Spanish, and Chileans after the independence of Chile from Spain in 1926. The Mapuche, among other Indigenous peoples, continue to resist through marches, hunger strikes, and social media campaigns; through advocating for policies and constitution recognition; and through promoting self-determination within national governing bodies, cultural revitalization, and coalition building with environmental and human rights organizations (Figueroa Huencho, 2021; Kowalczyk, 2013). The early class struggles manifested mostly through agriculture and mining, with workers often being in the center of resistance movements. In 1907 saltpeter miners went on strike because of working conditions and lack of pay. Many miners, with their wives and children, were shot to death in the northern city of Iquique by the Chilean army. Estrada (2007) states, "the Iquique killings came at the height of a spiral of massacres of workers unleashed by the Chilean state in 1903" (para. 15). Further, the 1973 coup produced the greatest massacre since 1907, also inspired by class resistance. Equally, women's resistance has been ongoing throughout Chilean history. Chilean women began the suffrage movement in 1845, and after a long struggle, they finally received full

80 · CHAPTER 4

political rights in 1949 (Pernet, 2000; Tagle, 2006). Women's resistance has encompassed a wide range of issues depending on race, class, and gender, among others. Thus, Chilean women have been a constant force throughout history in creating social change with diverse issues by way of being in solidarity, political organizing, and individual and collective activism.

Tomas and Poblaciónes

The *tomas de terrenos* (land occupations) that emerged in the 1950s and 1960s were in response to poverty and lack of affordable housing to address the growing working-class population in Santiago (Poblamiento, 2015). Some of the land occupations occurred in the outlying areas of Santiago and were organized by people of the impoverished sectors (Sepúlveda Swatson, 1998). Many of the *poblaciónes*[1] on the outskirts of Santiago today started as *tomas de terrenos*. At least two of the *poblaciónes* in Santiago where I conducted interviews began this way. On multiple occasions I was able to visit and speak with a few women who were part of the original organizers of a *toma de terreno* north of Santiago's city center. This *toma* began in the late 1960s as a result of dedicated organizing by young families who were members of the Communist Party. Five thousand families, often with very young children, were part of the original occupation. Maria Paz, who was part of the original occupation, told me that she was nineteen years old when she and her husband participated in the *toma*. In the early years of the *toma*, Salvador Allende, along with Pablo Neruda,[2] met with this community and offered both financial and structural support to develop housing and an infrastructure. Maria Paz told me that Pablo Neruda invited some of the young activists to his home in Isla Negra, a small pueblo by the ocean, and she was one of the activists invited. She told me that in the mornings they would talk about political issues and organizing, and in the evenings they would gather around music and poetry and would continue to discuss organizing strategies and politics. She shared that "a *toma* is a political act." Due to their commitment and efforts, Maria Paz and other women were instrumental in developing this intentional community focused on the health and well-being of families in the impoverished sector.

Because of their Communist affiliation and support of Allende, this community was heavily targeted with violence during the coup (Barbera, 2009). Mercedes, one of the original members of the *toma*, told me that the military government wanted war to extinguish the community. She told me that the community did not want violence, they just wanted change—housing, jobs, food, health care, and education—an agenda very different from the military's agenda. The same day as the coup, on September 11, 1973, the military police arrived in this community and restricted all freedom of movement (Madariaga Varela, 2010). Two days later began the *allanamientos* (searches), which lasted for years to come. Community members told me that the military forcibly removed males fourteen years and older and took them to another area of the *población*. The military would then question them, often detaining, torturing, or executing them. The youngest boy killed during the dictatorship was thirteen years old. Mercedes revealed, "the repression was very big here . . . many people died here, many people died in the street. It was a massacre." Despite the massive violence and repression toward this community, resistance to the dictatorship remained the central focus of organizing.

Organizing Under Military Repression

The violence and repression under the dictatorship destroyed any sense of normalcy in the lives of the women I spoke with who lived in the *poblaciónes*. Women were detained, tortured, sexually assaulted, and killed (Fried, 2006). Francesca remembers a girl, twenty years old, who was walking down the street in her *población* and killed by the military. Another girl was brutally tortured and raped while being detained. I met many women who shared memories of their experience during the dictatorship. On the 40th anniversary of the coup, I went to Londres 38, a memorial site that had been used as a detention and torture center. I met Elena on the street while we waited for the building to open. In the early 1970s, Elena was twenty years old when she was blindfolded and taken to Londres 38 by the military. When we got inside, she took me around and shared what she remembered of her time there. Some of the areas she wanted to show me were closed off with locked doors. In the areas that were open, she showed me where the machines were attached to the walls that administered electric shock, where she remembered a man lying on the floor, unmoving, and where they put the bodies when people died. She remembered the smell of urine in the air and the sounds of pain. Contrary to the politics of fear so widely practiced by authoritarian state repression under Pinochet, memories give meaning to the past (Sturken, 1997) and "can be empowering as well as healing for people who have been affected by state terrorism" (Barbera, 2009, p. 76). For women the politics of memory is "associated with women's silence, their apparent incapacity to speak about their experiences or to make sense of them within a social and cultural context" (Moenne, 2005, p. 153). Thus, memory is an act of resistance against silence and subordination. Paola shared that "without memory there is no context for [lived] experience." Elena's physical presence and recollection of memories at the site where she had been detained defied subjugation.

82 · CHAPTER 4

As the dictatorship primarily targeted, detained, or disappeared men, many women were left to navigate life on their own. Francesca remembers, "there was great suffering, very, very great suffering here. Everything deteriorated. This was our life." Francesca said it was difficult because most people were out of work during this time. People were hungry and had no food or money. In her *población*, she remembers several cases of women who were forced to trade sex for money to survive. Francesca said that as much as this time was about fear, it was also about resistance, "to survive at any cost." Francesca said:

> So, the people began to organize, especially women. It was the women who organized the children's home and the soup kitchens. It was the women who first started searching and reclaiming [family members] who were political prisoners, detainees, [and] disappeared. There was a strong resistance.

During the dictatorship of Pinochet, mothers and wives took to the streets to speak out against the torture and disappearance of their husbands and sons (Pieper Mooney, 2007). In a patriarchal system that structures gender inequity between men and women, defining women's experience as mothers and wives allows women to use mothering as a powerful political tool in destabilizing power and transforming political structures (Tibbetts, 1994). Patriarchy sees motherhood as non-political and less threatening, which not only allows women the freedom of social action but also legitimizes their demands as mothers and wives.

Pilar said, "*gracias a las mujeres*" (thanks to the women), the *población* where she lives was able to function during the dictatorship. Pilar said that women suffered a lot, in part because of the laws and social conditions that burdened women specifically. She said that women found strength with other women, and for Pilar, her mother was her first example of strength. Pilar's mother was a single mother of five children, after leaving her abusive husband. Many times Pilar's mother would defend other neighborhood women who were being beaten by their husbands. Mercedes shared that women in her community have always worked together. For example, since the beginning of the *toma*, women have addressed issues specific to their lived experience, such as intimate partner violence and health. Mercedes shared that women used to not have any rights, "everything for women was bad. They only existed to procreate and nothing else." In some ways, for Mercedes, there was almost no difference for women today. She said, "there are still women who are told by their husbands, 'hey dog, come' . . . it's terrible." During the dictatorship, Mercedes helped to organize and participate in a health group. This group organized around food and childcare, and it advocated for structural changes to address health issues in their community. This group also engaged in popular education, a method of critical consciousness-raising by those most impacted by inequity. They found ways to organize against the dictatorship and continue to organize around women's health issues. Mercedes reflected, "*la lucha no es en vano*" (the struggle is not in vain). Her ongoing solidarity work within her community has given her a lot of satisfaction. Mercedes said, "I fought a lot [and] I suffered." However, she is very grateful for what she has and said that these things you cannot forget, because "they are not things that you put out your hand and someone gives you, these are things that you had to fight for."

Women's Rights

Some of the participants I spoke with have been organizing around women's rights since the dictatorship. For example, Isadora and Paola, both feminist activists working at NGOs, were actively involved in the leftist movement during Allende and continued to organize through the period of the dictatorship. Isadora said that Allende's socialist proposal looked at women, for the first time, "not only as mothers and spouses, but also as workers . . . so the idea of having socialism and women going in to the workforce, it was possible to change the power relationships." She shared that it was during the dictatorship that a movement for women's rights began to develop.

Paola recalled one of Allende's speeches where he remarked, "all you women, [you] will be starting at the university, you will be a professional tomorrow, but you will have to go now and help women with the children." She shared that women's place in the leftist movement was very clear, as a traditional place in the home. With the types of social demands happening before and during Allende (1970–1973), Paola said, "they have no gender dimensions at all." She remembers sewing patches on the clothes, "*por los compañeros*" (for the comrades). Paola added, "we were part of more than one revolution, but we were women! And women had this space to work, but not [surpassing] the traditional roles." Paola remembered Allende using the term "the popular family" in his speeches. Built into the concept of the popular family, Paola shared, was the idea of men going to work all day and the women staying at home. She said:

> That's why women are the most important to support, for example, health policies. Taking children to the health programs . . . those programs are very successful, but they rely on women's time, they stand on women's time, women's time for the family, not for them[selves].

With the arrival of the dictatorship and the authoritarian regime, it was not difficult for the women I spoke with to see the connection between the control of women in society and the control of women within the home. Isadora shared:

84 · CHAPTER 4

> In the dictatorship we became more aware [that] what was going on in the country was so similar to the women's condition in the private space and so there is a change in Latin America. If you look at the feminist movement, it's a socialist movement. It's very strongly linked to social justice. It's very difficult to separate the women's condition with the social conditions as a whole. And so in the dictatorship was born the feminist movement. By the end of the 1970s . . . we had a strong women's movement.

According to Pieper Mooney and Campbell (2009):

> Women not only protested the military state, but also began to address domestic oppression in new ways: they recognized that the authoritarian . . . practices used by the regime to control the public sphere resembled those employed by men to control women in the private sphere. (p. 9)

Paola said, "That's why the motto that we had was, *democracia en el país y [democracia] en la casa* [democracy in the country and democracy in the home]." She agreed that it was easy to make the connection between the dictatorship in the country and at home. She said:

> The connection can be easily made when you look at the conditions with all women during these conflict situations. Women who didn't work had to work. Women who were unemployed had to reinvent themselves . . . they had to decide many, many, many things.

Paola shared that women went into the workforce, not because they were rebelling against the idea of staying at home, but because of the economic crisis in the 1980s, which made women's income necessary for the home. Paola said:

> So [women] have to go. And that means it's very hard for them to get into the work market, but also hard to get into work as it was hard to arrange [going to work] with domestic issues [at home] because they don't have the possibility of women to take care of [their children] like we have in the middle to higher class, that doesn't happen here in Chile.

Paola said that when women entered the workforce, they began to meet other women and share their realities of receiving low salaries and of conditions in the home, including domestic violence. Paola said that this was the first time many of these women had had these conversations. She explained:

> They talked for the first time . . . in women's spaces. So, I am absolutely sure that in the conditions like the ones we had during the dictatorship, where all spaces were closed . . . and they couldn't speak very much and they couldn't get

organized very much [that] that was very well processed by women to realize [their] condition.

Paola said that for women to see themselves outside of the home, reflect on their lives and their social position, and be able to share this with other women was empowering. Women began to develop a sense of shared experience, which produced an internal shift of critical consciousness (Freire, 1985; Pieper Mooney & Campbell, 2009).

Isadora remembers that during the dictatorship, the women's movement consisted of women across class backgrounds, which included diverse women's organizations, political parties, human rights groups, and neighborhood and grassroots organizations. Isadora said, "When we were walking together . . . the most important goal was to recover democracy. It was impossible to figure out how to change the conditions for women without changing the political regime." Thus, women from diverse backgrounds were working together for a common cause, to reclaim democracy.

By the return to democracy in 1990, there was a strong women's movement in Chile. Isadora explained that women wanted democracy, but they also wanted to be in the government to work on public policies. *Servicio Nacional de la Mujer* (SERNAM, National Women's Service) was established in 1991 to address the social, economic, and political discrimination against women (Richards, 2005). SERNAM was developed within a conservative and progressive political battleground, which shaped the particular scope that the organization embraced, resulting in an ideological emphasis on women's traditional role in the family and a structural condition limiting government resources. However, Isadora shared that "in twenty years, you can see how much we have advanced. What we've gained really, it was a cultural change." Despite SERNAM's limitations, the organization has been instrumental in passing key laws, such as legislation on domestic violence, divorce, and "workplace protections for pregnant women" (Blofield & Haas, 2005; Richards, 2005, p. 7).

Paola remembers municipalities working to build women's centers after the return to democracy, which she said discounted much of the women's movement that had been established during the dictatorship. She recalled:

> They tried to build women's centers instead of supporting the ones that women had been doing during the dictatorship. That should have been wonderful! There was a whole generation of women leadership in the *población*. Everywhere, not only in the *poblaciónes*, [also] in the university [were] women leaders who were able to create a lot of things, and what happens? They say, "no, this is from the municipality and that's yours."

Paola shared that this was disempowering for women not to receive recognition after working in solidarity for many years during the dictatorship across race and class lines. Richards (2004) states that SERNAM's emphasis on individual rights for women disregards Indigenous women's identity, experience, and struggle for collective rights. Rayen, a Mapuche woman who works for an Indigenous organization, shared that the government mainly offers resources to Mapuche women around cultural development, rather than supporting the socio-political realities that Mapuche women face. Rayen said there is no political advancement for Mapuche women, as there is no space to have a voice in political participation. Further, by only focusing on gender issues, SERNAM excludes race and class concerns for women in the *poblaciónes* and *campamentos*. This lack of representation from government organizations reflects the power inequity of and among women in the general society (Richards, 2005). Thus, it is equally important to highlight the ways resistance is reproduced, challenged, and sustained in marginalized spaces.

Bodies in Protest

May 1, 2014, marked a national holiday in honor of the *trabajadores* and *trabajadoras* (workers), aligning with International Workers' Day.[3] On this day, the trade unions organize rallies all over Chile to speak out in support of the rights of workers and the current issues they face. Billboards with faces of legislative representatives honoring workers showed national support. Schools, government offices, and many stores were closed in honor and recognition of workers and as is the tradition, for workers to convene and exercise their rights. Plaza Brasil, a neighborhood in the center of Santiago, was filled with people—children, families, elders, the working class, artists, students, lawyers—a very diverse group. In the middle of the plaza was a stage where union representatives gave their speeches and music and spoken word artists performed. Many people were selling food, clothing, music, and art. It was an empowering space to gather in solidarity with others.

As I was listening to a union representative reading a list of demands of workers' rights, addressed to the current Bachelet government, a vein of the crowd started running in full force through the middle of the plaza, like a stretch of a river set free after a dam breaks. It was the sound of running that first caught my attention. I barely had time to register what was going on before I was body-slammed by a desperate runner in search of a safe place to be, and there was none. Then I saw a group of *carabiñeros* (special police force considered to be a branch of the armed forces) in army green wearing helmets and carrying shields and battalions, the full regalia, running behind the civilians. I felt as if I were in the middle of a war zone: people running in fear, tear gas filling the plaza, police shooting rubber bullets into the crowd from the surrounding buildings, and armored tanks shooting high-pressure water into the mass.

What I saw and experienced on the first of May in Chile was complete disrespect for human rights. Disrespect for the rights of workers, who can legally demonstrate around their struggle for livable wages, among other unequal conditions. Disrespect for the safety of the general population, as the force and pursuance of the *carabiñeros* created an extremely violent and unsafe environment for everyone, including children, in the plaza that day. A blatant disregard for public health and safety, particularly women's reproductive health, was evident in the use of tear gas, which can cause serious harm, including causing spontaneous abortion. This is ironic considering Chile's stance on abortion at the time. According to the 1993 Chemical Weapons Convention, tear gas has been banned in warfare due to the high toxicity and negative health effects (Larsson, 2020). Although tear gas has been banned in warfare, it is still used in domestic policing. Also, the *carabiñeros* were grabbing all young people with cell phones and throwing them into the modern-day military paddy wagon. One young man, who looked no more than twenty years old, was using his cell phone when he was encircled by five *carabiñeros* much bigger than him. He was hit with a baton and taken away, a completely unnecessary use of force. At another point a tank entered the plaza and was spraying high-pressured water over the back of and onto the stage, halting the performance that was taking place. The event ended without any closure whatsoever. Everyone was in survival mode and the *carabiñeros* encircled and closed off the plaza.

As we were dispersing, a woman told me that the violence happening on that day reminded her of the violence she experienced on the streets during the dictatorship. Thus, the people in the plaza gathering in solidarity with the working class became the target of police repression and violence, similar to the type of repressive control experienced during the dictatorship. The struggle of and the impact on working-class bodies are not much different between historical and contemporary time periods. Adair (2001) states that power holds on to bodies in ways that "physically inscribe . . . punish, and display" defiant bodies as dangerous. Resistance occurs within and is in response to inequity, so "consequences of resistance often lead to further oppression and domination" (Caputo, 2014, p. 14).

Within such a repressive environment, other bodies in protest resorted to a more radical approach. Katia, an activist with a lesbian and feminist collective, said they are activists of the street. They make masks and march naked to raise awareness about abortion, she said, "with all body types." They also make "bombs [balloons] with menstrual blood." When I asked whether it was symbolic or real blood, Katia smiled and answered, "some symbolic, some real." She explained that they are reflecting societal messaging about women's bodies: "we are very disgusting bodies," she said. In this way, they are reclaiming their power by transforming the internalization of shame into personal and collective power when in solidarity with other women. When I asked her how she feels when she is protesting with blood or without clothes, she said, "fantastic. It's a power. A strong sensation." Different cultures and women's groups have used naked bodies as a protest strategy throughout history. For example, in Kenya, the *guturamira ng'ania*, to curse a person by stripping, is a pre-colonial method of resistance available to Kikuyu women (Tibbetts, 1994). Salime (2014) explains, "nudity places the body on deliberate display [and] converts the shame associated with the naked body into shame associated with gazing and touching" (p. 15). Thus, many women use their naked bodies as a form of reclamation against various forms of gender oppression. Katia said that Chile is "*tan reprimido*" (very repressed), so they want to show their bodies, the blood, the pain, to highlight social difference. She said, "Because abortion is the crystallization, it is a manifestation of the most unequal level in society."

A phenomenon in Chile that I witnessed regarding public spaces of contestation is how diverse the groups are that are coming together to put their bodies on the line in protest. Diverse in age, gender, sexuality, political affiliation, class background, physical ability, education level, professions, and organizations, many people came together to create change. When I participated in a march to decriminalize abortion, I approached a group of men who looked to be in their twenties, walking in the march and holding Che Guevara flags. I asked one of them why they were participating in a protest to decriminalize abortion, and he told me they were there to be in solidarity with women. He told me that the same system that denies women's rights creates and sustains inequity across diverse issues within the country. Similarly, during one of my research trips to Chile, many students had occupied their universities, and classes were canceled for almost a year. I interviewed a student inside the University of Chile about why he was in a *toma* there. Students at top universities usually are from middle- to upper-income households, so I was curious why he was negotiating and fighting for free and quality education for all Chileans, as this did not apply specifically to him or his peers at the university. He told me that he was there because he had a social conscience. He said, "I feel I have a responsibility to my country to make it a better one. And I think a lot of people feel the same."

Collective Spaces

Various forms of resistance were revealed within women's collective spaces, outside of mainstream government institutions. These ranged from feminist and women's organizations to grassroots neighborhood committees or gatherings. Women addressed issues of violence against women, the decriminalization of abortion, health and reproductive health, political leadership and participation, community development, and a hotline to assist women with using misoprostol appropriately. The strategies of women's resistance include organized marches, workshops, meetings, events, street education, and body expression. Women used popular education; radio; murals and other art forms; publication materials, such as pamphlets, manuals, leaflets, and flyers; and informal group discussions. Paz recalled participating in a women's group: "I know a lot of women who are organizing . . . and I participate in some discussions that I'm interested in and it's growing, it's beautiful." Sutton (2005) states, "both political protest and daily activist work demand intense *bodily* commitment . . . [and] is about engaging other bodies in the project of creating social change, of building power together from the bottom up" (p. 176). Thus, in addition to the separate collective spaces of resistance revealed in this study, collectively, these organizations and grassroots groups and committees support each other in solidarity to resist oppressive structures. Further, groups network with each other. For example, the lesbian and feminist collective that Katia is a part of often networks with other groups to bring knowledge of using misoprostol appropriately to marginalized spaces that normally would not have access to this information. Katia explained that groups reach out to them and, in turn, they conduct workshops in various areas with Mapuche women, immigrant women, women in poverty, and women who are sex workers.

Women's collective spaces seemed to occur naturally based on similar interests, experience, and personal commitment and responsibility to resist dominant cultural expectations and gender norms. For example, Macarena shared that it is important for her to reclaim her rights as a woman. She reflected:

> I have many problems in this society because when I [see] that somebody is abusing a woman . . . I can't be quiet, immediately I go . . . "no, you can't say that" or "'you can't do that with this person." I feel more affinity with women, of course, it's my first group of reference in my life.

When women shared their struggles with identity, sexuality, or place in society, they indicated that they wanted to give back to society, specifically to women so

90 • CHAPTER 4

that other women would have a different experience. Esperanza discussed the fear she had around her sexuality. The thought of being sexual produced panic. Now her perspective has shifted, and she thinks many young women who are fourteen or fifteen years old have sex, but they do not realize the value of their sexuality. She said, "It's an expression, very beautiful. Sexuality with or without love, it's good, but it's not seen this way." Esperanza now understands the context in which her fear was embedded. She named the Catholic Church as the principal cause of shame and fear around her sexuality. However, Esperanza has transformed her fear into resistance against the dominant cultural expectation of women by reclaiming her sexuality as beautiful and not shameful. Now, she says, it is important to teach other women, especially young women. She said, "women have value, [but] many women don't think this in Chile. . . . [We] need to teach women . . . [there] is no need to be afraid."

On numerous occasions I had the opportunity to be with women in collective spaces, and each time I witnessed solidarity among women and a strong sense of belonging, especially within the communities that I visited on more than one occasion. To have a place to gather among women felt like a sacred space, and I was grateful to be included. In the south of Chile, I was invited to celebrate the Mapuche New Year with a community that I had visited multiple times. The Mapuche embrace a collective identity connected to *la naturaleza* (nature). There is not a focus on the self, as Rayen described earlier, but rather a consciousness about the collective, which is part of a worldview of interconnectedness. The Mapuche New Year aligns with the winter solstice in the southern hemisphere; thus, it is a celebration of the new sun. The celebration included traditional Mapuche food, ritual, and dance. The food was homemade, such as the *masa* (dough) for the empanadas, tortillas, and bread, the latter baked in the hot ash and residual embers from the fire. The process of making food was intentional and gradual, coming together over a two-day period. Making food for such an event is a ritual conducted mostly by women. When women arrived at the gathering, they immediately went to the kitchen or to the fire where food was being made. It is a time for women to be together and to create something for the community. Over this two-day cooking period, I was struck by and felt very much a part of community with women. We sat around the fire in the *ruka*, a traditional Mapuche house, making food, sometimes drinking wine, and constantly talking, sharing various topics, such as sex, having babies, relationships, and violence in the home. We laughed, we cried, and we continued to cook. Having had this opportunity, I understood the importance of collective spaces for women to be with each other. It is a sacred space, one that happens naturally and instinctively in this environment.

The existence of collective spaces for women within the larger context of race, class, and gender inequity demonstrates resistance in the way of carving out a safe place to have a voice and a sense of belonging. These collective spaces represent mutual aid networks where women support each other. Developing mutual aid networks within the context of highly restrictive environments is an act of resistance. Thus, women create collective spaces as a form of resistance against types of violence that constrain power and agency (Parkins, 2000).

Networks of Solidarity

Participants discussed the significance of social networks as a form of resistance in responding to women's need to obtain a clandestine abortion in the context of illegality. Positive social networks provided access to needed information, support, and some level of trust within clandestine spaces. Participants shared that these were part of feminist, women's, and political networks or just formed through word of mouth among friends or acquaintances.

According to Maira, Hurtado, & Santana (2010), "feminists have always created clandestine networks of solidarity to facilitate women's access to safe abortion" (p. 31). This was highlighted in the experience of two participants. Anaís mentioned that she found out about the private clinic she went to for two of her abortions through a feminist network. Anaís was part of a feminist collective, and this is how she had access to information, through a friend in the collective. Pía had a similar experience, being referred by someone she trusted. She reflected:

> I went to a *matrona* who worked in human rights, she took me to a place where a colleague of hers did these abortions . . . I trusted in her, she was a *matrona* and this was a colleague of hers . . . I didn't know her, but [I had] this sort of trust in this woman because her name was given by another one who I respect, [so] I knew she worked in the same things that I did.

Francesca talked about constructing a network among women, but she did not identify it as a feminist network. She said:

> Suddenly we just need to know, and we started to talk and there were those who knew the information. [So] we started to talk to that person [about] how we do it and we had to go through that person, and that person took the girl to the person . . . who would do the abortion. One does not know more than that, . . . There were also constructed networks where we got money together [for women to go to places] not as expensive as a clinic.

92 · CHAPTER 4

Macarena's boyfriend at the time of her first pregnancy was part of an organized group called the Communist Youth of Chile, so she discovered where to go through a political network. She revealed:

> It was the early '90s, just after the *plebicito* [vote], after people say [they] don't want Pinochet in the government . . . we [were] very involved in the political issues, my family, all my family. My grandfather was in the jail for many years, political prisoner, and we come from the exile, like three years before, so we [were] very involved in the political issues in the country, . . . I remember that my partner was . . . part of the *Juventudes Comunistas* [Communist Youth] and so he had more networks in Chile. He started to ask some close friends, [male] friends, and one of them [said], "well, we know a doctor, a woman doctor, who made abortions . . . " and so it's [a] woman from the *Partido Comunista* [Communist Party] who [did the abortion].

Other women had found how to access an abortion through friends who had gone through the same experience. In fact, most of the women I spoke with who shared their abortion experience with me said that after their abortion, they supported other women in some way. Thus, much of the solidarity that women had with other women came out of their own experience of not having the kind of support that they needed at the time. Pía remembered helping a young woman through her abortion experience:

> We worked together, she might have been twenty-one, or twenty . . . I remember feeling like sort of *with* among women, going with her to the clinic, bringing her back to say at my home because she couldn't go to her house because she lived with her mother and with the family and trying to be *with* her, letting her sleep, or making her something to drink or whatever it was. . . . I think that's one of the points where women can be or show solidarity with other women.

Paz had said that she found out about misoprostol from a friend who had used misoprostol to terminate her pregnancy. Paz felt that going through an illegal abortion served a purpose because she recently helped a friend who was going through the same experience. She helped her friend do research on where to find misoprostol as well as helped her make contact to get the pills. She said in that moment, she had the role of a counselor or support person for her friend, which is something that she did not have herself. Paz explained to her friend, "OK, don't worry, in the next day you will feel this . . . you will do that, you can do these things or other things to feel better, you know, like trying to explain everything."

Macarena had a similar experience. She explained that a few months after her abortion, she was helping her classmates in the same situation.

> I remember two or three friends in my classroom have an abortion and I felt like the more mature woman next to them because I had the experience . . . and I started to support friends that are living the same situation. . . . One of the best things I did in my life, a good experience, was [to] support other women when they were pregnant. I think that made me feel useful in my life because I passed [through] that situation, I felt bad, I needed help, and to be part of these groups was very, very useful . . . you know, [in] all these situations when I think to be one of these women the only thing that I have in my mind is they need to talk with somebody—they need information, they need support, they need to feel that they are not the only person that [has] that problem.

Pia said, "It's the link among women that can help us." There was a strong sense of solidarity among women that occurred naturally. In addressing *testimonio*, personal narratives based on oral traditions in Latin America, Bernal, Burciaga & Carmona (2012) state that sharing personal stories helps to break through silences and create solidarity, "situating the individual in communion with a collective experience marked by marginalization [and] oppression. . . . " (p. 363). Thus, it is in the collective experience that women find solidarity and a sense of purpose in helping other women. In fact, Paz mentioned this as the reason why she wanted to participate in an interview for this study. She said that she was interested in participating to change the narrative from rage and hate. She reflected:

> I don't want to be afraid to explore myself because this exploration can help another person. So I want to be here in this [interview] for me, and all the women, or boys, or [people], that have questions about this subject. It's a beautiful subject because it's another way to understand the function of life. Thank you for making me talk about this.

Paz, like other women, needed a space to communicate her embodied reality of abortion in the context of criminalization. In this way, Paz demonstrates how participating in an interview was an act of resistance. The illegal and clandestine nature of abortion alone is enough to perpetuate fear, silence, and isolation in women. Thus, when women are able to connect with other women, this helps deconstruct the dominant cultural discourse on abortion. Similar to feminist consciousness-raising groups in the 1970s, when women foster collective spaces in the margins, they "become aware that the problems they thought were theirs

94 • CHAPTER 4

alone are less a function of their own personal hangups than of the social structure and culture in which they live" (Polk, 1972, p. 324).

Conclusion

This chapter revealed Chile's culture of race, class, and gender resistance against oppressive laws, ideologies, and practices, including the ways in which women embody resistance in the context of restrictive and clandestine spaces. Just as women's identities and abortion experiences are defined by multiple interlocking systems of oppression, so is the potential for contestation within these systems. Thus, the body is a site of inequity and resistance simultaneously across time and social location (Caputo, 2010). No matter the risk in the face of inequity, repression, or marginalization, women's capacity to resist was constant. Embodying resistance, as Sutton (2005) explains, occurs with the whole self, and therefore, "to create more equitable, just, and humane societies, we need to take into account the bodily worlds of marginalized populations" (p. 191).

Conclusion

Revelations from Chile

> Criminal laws penalizing and restricting induced abortion are the paradigmatic examples of impermissible barriers to the realization of women's right to health and must be eliminated.
>
> —UN Special Rapporteur on the Right to Health, 2011, p. 7

The complexity of abortion, born out of and continually situated within multiple systems of inequity, is not unique to Chile. This phenomenon exists across geographic boundaries. The challenges revealed and insights gained in Chile can be extended to other countries, contexts, and populations, especially in regard to naming, deconstructing, and ideally dismantling structures of violence that determine reproductive health experiences. Centering women and other pregnant people is critical to guide what we understand and know about abortion. Centering people who are most harmed by restrictive laws and policies counters the dismissive and violent *otherizing* of dominant discourses, advancing a social justice approach to knowledge production. As Mohanty (2003) states, "I believe that this experiential and analytic anchor in the lives of marginalized communities of women provides the most inclusive paradigm for thinking about social justice" (p. 231). There is a lot to unpack from the experiences shared during the course of this research. What follows is certainly not an exhaustive list, but rather an invitation to explore more deeply some of the key areas that were revealed. For this reason and others, it is critical to continue to reframe the criminalization of abortion as the criminalization of women for abortion, highlighting the concrete impact on women who are constructed as criminals.

Criminalization

Criminalization produces a narrow lens from which to understand the social issues surrounding women's reproductive health. This results in unnecessary harm by placing the onus of responsibility on individuals, subsequently fostering a permissive discriminatory environment. One of the problems with linking abortion to a criminal act is that it "decontextualizes women from the social and political parameters of their lives" (Pollack, 2000, p. 79). This approach situates the underlying cause of criminality as individual responsibility rather than the construction of laws and policies that do not take into account the conditions of inequity as a contributing factor when terminating a pregnancy.

Centering the analysis on the narratives of women, whose reproductive lives are embedded within a web of restrictive policies and practices, offers insight into what it means to be criminalized. Participant narratives revealed how laws and policies that criminalize women for terminating a pregnancy do not take into consideration the broader issues of race, class, and gender inequity in which these policies are constructed, resulting in further social, economic, and political disparities for women already marginalized in Chilean society. This study highlighted how restrictive reproductive laws and policies disproportionately target and regulate the lives of poor, Indigenous, and immigrant women.

Tracing reproductive health policies and practices over three distinct time periods, pre-1973 coup d'état, during the seventeen-year dictatorship, and after the return to democracy, underscores the ongoing nature of and need for abortion. Deciding to terminate a pregnancy, by itself, is not a criminal act. It is laws and policies within specific political climates that construct women as criminals. This piece is critical to understand. Women are not somehow inherently bad or wrong. It is the context in which abortion, gender inequity, and related policies and practices are framed and sustained that harms women. A critical aspect of abortion that places a significant burden on women is the political climate, which includes cultural and social discourse, as well as the laws and policies. Together, these forces can create a context of empowerment or, in this case, marginalization, where women are systematically limited in their ability to fully participate in and influence social, political, and economic spaces.

The necessity of abortion is undeniable. It has always existed and will continue to be a crucial aspect of women's reproductive health and rights, especially in the context of social, economic, and political inequity. Rather than protecting women, restrictive reproductive health policies target women, which gives permission to treat them poorly in the systems of health, education, and the law, among others. Thus, women are forced to navigate multiple layers of institutional discrimination and spaces of violence against them. Adding to an already overwhelming situation is the unjust sense of responsibility placed on women for their actions, projecting blame for the moral ills of society. In truth, the societal context is inherently flawed, and it shapes women's experiences. As Macarena shared, "the traumatized situation comes from the context, not the abortion." This deep-rooted issue is a form of violence that is complex and multifaceted, making it difficult to address directly. Women can lose themselves within these narratives, internalizing oppression rather than their own authentic identities, which perpetuates the construct of marginalization and disempowerment.

Also, criminalizing women for abortion creates clandestine spaces and promotes a black-market economy. Women are forced into unsafe conditions, putting their health and lives at risk. Participants shared that clandestine spaces produced fear, restricted agency, and silenced their voice, consequently invisibilizing their experience. As Pía shared after the coup d'état, the secrecy surrounding abortion was unlike anything she had ever experienced. She moved through spaces that did not exist and realized how much more silencing the experience of abortion was, compared to her clandestine political work during the dictatorship. While her political work against the dictatorship involved significant risk, the experience of seeking a clandestine abortion took place within her body, a deeply personal experience, intensified by the overwhelming silence that surrounded it.

The experiences that women shared about navigating clandestine spaces were deeply profound. If the clandestine spaces did not exist, then neither did their experiences within these spaces. Thus, if women's abortion experience does not have a place to exist, then the state can give it the place it wants. Highlighting women's narratives exposes state violence and unearths the silences, offering a counternarrative to repressive state policies and cultural discourse. In response to the social exclusion and marginalization in which women's lives are reduced, centering women's narratives fosters a space of critical reflection to make visible harmful power structures and contestation, acknowledging the strength of women's resistance within the context of repressive environments. Mohanty (2003) states, "This particular marginalized location makes the politics of knowledge and the power investments that go along with it visible so that we can then engage in work to transform the use and abuse of power" (p. 231).

The social isolation that women who terminate a pregnancy in a highly criminalized environment experience is exacerbated by the lack of support and protection from professionals and the state. The professionals in *consultorios* I interviewed stated they did not broach the abortion dialogue with women because

98 · *Conclusion*

of abortion's illegality and clandestine nature at the time. This illustrates how structural and cultural violence play a significant role in regulating and limiting the capacity of helping professions. Some professionals feared retribution from the state, a carryover from the Pinochet dictatorship, and for others the fear was in the reaction of their colleagues. During the Pinochet dictatorship people who spoke out were tortured, and others disappeared. Helping professionals are also vulnerable to the laws and policies constructed within a specific political climate. This has serious ethical policy and practice implications for health professions, among others, whose base value is to alleviate human suffering.

Unpacking Inequity

Developing a critical theoretical framework is a requisite when unpacking complex systems of inequity and their impact on lived experience. Frameworks offer a way to see, understand, and name what is happening as well as guide resistance, solidarity, and change efforts. A combination of various theoretical frameworks was constructed to create a prism-like lens that aided in unpacking inequity in its complexity. Framing inequity as indivisible from lived experience highlighted the ways women navigate their reproductive lives in a complex system of distinct, interlocking forms of oppression. Women's stories illustrated how their voices and experiences with abortion are silenced in the context of illegality, becoming visible only when health issues or legal consequences emerge. A critical analysis of how illegality is inscribed on a woman's body and embodied reality helped to link broader constructs of violence to lived experience. Women revealed the ways in which everyday violence impacts their lives, and through their narratives, we can better understand how their experience is profoundly interconnected to and shaped by laws, policies, institutions, and cultural discourse. The multidimensional framework helps to recognize and make visible women's embodied existence as they defined it within the narratives of their abortion experience.

The way in which Galtung's (1990) typology of violence was applied aided as a model to identify and deconstruct multiple forms of inequity. Structural violence helped to situate the construction of laws and policies in historic and contemporary economic and political processes that regulate and control women's reproductive lives and construct them as criminals. Cultural violence facilitated an understanding of how systems of inequity are legitimized and sustained, reinforcing permissive harmful attitudes and practices toward young, poor, Indigenous, and immigrant women. Direct violence illustrated how structural and cultural violence manifest as concrete expressions of discrimination and emotional, sexual, and physical violence against women. Together, these offer a holistic framework to carry out a comprehensive analysis of the constraint on women's agency, in which their reproductive lives and experiences are embedded.

What makes a woman more susceptible to the typology of violence is her social location. Thus, adding intersectionality to this framework helps to shed light on the multiple ways that structures of inequity shape women's reproductive lives. Paloma, for example, suffered multiple forms of discrimination, as a Peruvian immigrant, a domestic worker, and a woman. The categories of race, class, gender, and nation determined Paloma's vulnerability to structural, cultural, and direct violence broadly, and specifically limited agency concerning her reproductive health decisions and experience. Intersectionality highlights how restrictive reproductive health policies do not impact women equally; they criminalize certain women for not having access to resources or the ability to move freely within the constraints of their social location. Bringing together the typology of violence with intersectionality clearly exposes restrictive reproductive health policies as connected to broader issues of social injustice and human rights violations.

The United Nations Special Rapporteur on the Right to Health (2011) highlights that the denial of access to services and information, gender inequity and discrimination, and the marginalization of women and girls when they are denied their right to sexual and reproductive health further exacerbate human rights harms. The rapporteur states, "Public morality cannot serve as a justification for enactment or enforcement of laws that may result in human rights violations, including those intended to regulate sexual and reproductive conduct and decision-making" (p. 7). Specific to abortion, the rapporteur addresses the criminalization of abortion as a violation of a woman's right to be free from inhumane and cruel treatment, to have control over her body, and to be free from the conditions that are created from a black-market economy surrounding abortion, such as exploitation and violence. These violations of human rights are highlighted in this study through women's narratives of abortion experience within the context of illegality. Including a human rights framework elevates the rights of women, rather than criminalizing women for what is constructed as immoral behavior. The interrelationship of human rights with reproductive health, specific to abortion, is complex and multifaceted, encompassing the right to health, autonomy and bodily integrity, gender equity, non-discrimination, and socioeconomic and legal rights. It provides a deeper understanding of geographic and culturally specific contexts. Ensuring access to safe and legal abortion services is crucial not only for individual well-being but also toward the realization of human rights broadly. By centering the voices and experiences of those most harmed by restrictive reproductive policies, we can see that reproductive freedom can be achieved when individuals have the resources and structural supports to make choices free from coercion, discrimination, and oppression.

Revisiting Choice

The risk associated with having a clandestine abortion, such as the threat to women's health and lives, necessitates an examination of how we understand choice. No woman in this study chose to put her life at risk. In the context of contemporary debates on abortion, "choice" implies a certain degree of personal and political agency or free will. The stories that women in this study shared revealed that many of them feel they do not have choice about their bodies. For women who are economically, politically, and socially marginalized, their body is not their own. Some women voiced a sense that their bodies belong to the state, as the state controls health care access and dictates whether they are forced to seek unsafe, clandestine abortions. The women who worked as domestic workers felt their body was owned by their employer, who decided how many hours they worked, whose children they raised, and whether they would lose their job if they became pregnant. Immigrant women who put their bodies at risk when crossing borders, hiding their bodies, trafficking drugs in exchange for entry into the country, or not working legally, were reminded how vulnerable they were to exploitation and abuse at the hands of others. In clandestine spaces, women shared that not having a voice or agency in relation to their bodies created a sense of isolation, exclusion, and a lack of belonging or feeling that they had a place in society. Other women who faced reproductive oppression in public health institutions during the dictatorship and after the return to democracy expressed that the absence of consent and the lack of inclusion in decision-making reinforced the feeling that their bodies were not their own. Women in violent relationships shared feeling disconnected to their bodies and sense of self as their male partners controlled their reproduction and general mobility, or lack thereof.

Racism and other forms of oppression—whether through structural, cultural, or direct violence—intersect in ways that significantly compound the challenges women face across various dimensions of their lives. Systemic inequities, deeply ingrained in laws, policies, and institutional practices, create barriers that limit access to essential resources and services. These inequities manifest not only in discriminatory laws but also in the everyday operations of institutions that are supposed to support and protect women. The perpetuation of stereotypes and biases contribute to a societal narrative that devalues women, particularly those from historically marginalized backgrounds. Such narratives are reinforced through media representations, cultural norms, and historic injustices that shape public perception and treatment of these women. When societal structures fail to recognize women's worth and agency, they create an environment in which women feel unsafe, not valued, not welcome, or that they do not have a place in society. Consequently, these dynamics and practices undermine women's ability to engage in decision-making processes—not only for themselves but also for their families and communities.

The narratives of these women revealed that the decision to terminate a pregnancy most often was connected to concerns about motherhood and family. Thus, abortion is about motherhood and family more than it is not. For example, Macarena was breastfeeding her baby girl during our interview. She discussed the importance of being able to provide a loving and secure environment with two parents, which she was not able to do as a single teen mom. Paloma was the primary financial provider and emotional support for her four children. Her husband was an alcoholic and extremely abusive. Paloma had no control within her relationship to manage family planning. Nor did she have control in her work environment when her *patrona* told her that if she became pregnant, she would lose her job. Keeping her job to support her children meant that Paloma could not become pregnant again. Yet Paloma had no control within her relationship of whether she became pregnant. Paloma's decision to terminate her pregnancies, like the decisions of other women interviewed for this study, was in response to the economic and social inequity in which her life and the context of her decisions are embedded. The dominant cultural discourse on abortion in Chile declares that women who terminate their pregnancies have acted against the social norm of being a mother. Francisco observed that mainstream society struggles to accept abortion, because it is difficult to envision a woman who does not want to become a mother. However, it is often women's commitment to motherhood that makes abortion the forced alternative.

Resistance in the Margins

Marginality is not only a place of exclusion, but also a place of resistance, situating the body as a site of simultaneous control and contestation (Foucault, 1977, 1990; Hollander & Einwohner, 2004; Wade, 1997). Despite many barriers navigating inequity in clandestine spaces, women revealed resistance to dominant

102 · *Conclusion*

structures, laws, and cultural discourse, illustrating individual and collective forms of agency. The narratives of women illustrated how women's bodies were marked by race, class, and gender inequity within clandestine spaces of illegality. And women disclosed a parallel reality, revealing the power to act within highly restrictive environments. Resistance takes many forms, and the root act— however loud or subtle—is being in opposition to oppression. Resistance efforts are critical to recognize and elevate in the face of harmful, repressive laws and practices. It is this resistance that moves us forward toward just reproductive policies and practices. Chile offers valuable insights about resistance efforts. Among these are the importance of recognizing power and agency in women, identifying the multifaceted forms of women's resistance, and cultivating a sense of solidarity and liberation in the collective pursuit of justice within and between geographic spaces.

Women shared narratives exposing the violence embedded in their lives, revealing a resistance to multiple forms of inequity and oppression. Neglecting to acknowledge the innate strength and resistance women display against oppressive systems and practices risks perpetuating a paternalistic culture and practice that invisbilizes women. This reductionist perspective oversimplifies complex issues and minimizes the impact of restrictive reproductive health barriers and challenges that women navigate. The purpose here is to underscore and elevate acts of resistance. Harmful dominant narratives take root due to the absence of counternarratives to challenge them. However, when the presence of structural, cultural, and direct violence can be clearly identified, it becomes evident that the responsibility does not rest with the individual, but rather with the environmental context that fosters such conditions. Further, when acts of resistance are seen and acknowledged in the face of this violence, it reduces the likelihood of internalizing oppression. This awareness can carve a path to liberation, and while it may not lead immediately to policy changes, it can alleviate self-blame and shift the responsibility for blame onto the systemic structures, cultural discourse, and individuals who perpetuate these conditions.

Recognizing the many ways that women demonstrate resistance is instrumental in dismantling the silence and invisibility surrounding their experiences. It is crucial, then, to recognize that the decision to terminate a pregnancy within a highly criminalized environment is an act of resistance. This was further revealed when women put their bodies in harm's way to obtain an illegal abortion, when women put themselves at risk to help other women, when women used their naked bodies to defy repressive cultural identity and expectations, when women engaged in traditional health practices, and when women protested in marches to contest injustice. Further, collective spaces of resistance

Conclusion • 103

formed because of the ways many women were harmed by the same systems of state-sanctioned inequity and violence, thus creating a network of solidarity. An intersectional lens is essential for highlighting how both individual and collective acts of resistance are situated in the context of repressive race, class, and gender inequity. Thus, recognizing and elevating resistance invites us to imagine the possibilities of different, more equitable ways of being in the world.

Framing women as criminals for seeking abortions is deeply intertwined with the political climate and societal context of the time, overshadowing the complex realities of women's lives and the inequities they face. Centering women and pregnant people at the forefront, to guide our knowledge and solidarity efforts, is an essential social justice approach that paves the way for reproductive health, human rights, and just policies and practices. Understanding and acknowledging the complexity of experiences and the multiple factors that determine decisions to terminate a pregnancy is essential for fostering a more just society where pregnant people can embody agency without fear of punishment or stigma. This book, in part, serves as a platform for bearing witness to and providing a collective and political space for the lived experience of women and others who shed light on the multiple harms within clandestine spaces of illegality.

Notes

Introduction

1. See https://www.womenonwaves.org/.

2. Each of the participants was given a pseudonym to protect their identity, while providing a more intimate and human connection with the stories shared.

3. In this case, the *toma* refers to the occupation or takeover of a university by students. Between 2011 and 2013, *tomas* were part of the student movement and happened in both private and public universities and high schools across Chile.

4. For a more comprehensive look at reproductive justice, see Gurr, 2015; Luna, 2020; Roberts, 2016; Ross & Solinger, 2017; Saroj Bakhru, 2019; Sillman & Bhattacharjee, 2002; Silliman, Fried, Ross, & Gutierrez, 2004; and Smith, 2005.

5. See Dejarlais, 1997; Dolezal & Petherbridge, 2017; Willen, 2007.

6. See Chapter 1.

7. See Chapter 2.

8. See Chapter 3.

9. See Crenshaw, 1991, 2017; Hill Collins, 2019; Hill Collins & Bilge, 2020.

10. *Poblaciónes* in Chile are communities or neighborhoods made up of low-income housing, where people in poverty and the working class live. They exist throughout the country, and some *poblaciónes* are more developed than others.

11. Neighborhood public health centers.

Chapter 1. Inequity

1. The conclusion of this study.

2. Illegitimacy is a gendered and sexist term and a pejorative birth label that has been used throughout history.

106 · *Notes*

3. 1989–2017.
4. See Sutton & Vacarezza (2021).
5. Derived from *tomar*, meaning "to take."

Chapter 2. Unpacking Inequity

1. Within a binary gender construct.
2. Misoprostol is used to prevent ulcers but also to induce labor.

Chapter 3. Centering Women

1. A hollow rubber tube placed in the cervix to allow air to enter the uterus.

Chapter 4. ¡Resistencia!

1. Communities in poverty.
2. Chilean poet and political activist; received the Nobel Peace Prize for Literature in 1971.
3. "Bodies in Protest" is based on Sutton's (2010) work on *poner el cuerpo*, which "means not just to talk, think, or desire, but to be really presented and involved; to put the whole (embodied) being into action . . . " (p. 161).

References

Abortion Policies: A Global Review (2001). Country profiles: Chile (pp. 92–93). United Nations Publication, Volume I. Retrieved from https://www.un.org/development/desa/pd/sites/www.un.org.development.desa.pd/files/files/documents/2021/Nov/undesa_pd_2001_abortion-policies-a-global-review-volume-i-afghanistan-to-france.pdf.

Adair, V. C. (2001). Branded with infamy: Inscriptions of poverty and class in the United States. *Journal of Women in Culture and Society, 27*(2), 451–471.

Allende, S. (2005). Medical and social reality in Chile. *International Journal of Epidemiology, 34,* 732–736. (Reprinted from La Realidad Médico-Social Chilena, Santiago, Chile. Ministerior de Salubridad, 1939).

Anglin, M. K. (1998). Feminist perspectives on structural violence. *Identities, 5*(2), 145–151.

Armijo, R., & Monreal, T. (1965). Epidemiology of provoked abortion in Santiago, Chile. *Journal of Sex Research, 1*(2), 143–149.

Ashford, L. S. (2004, September 14). What was Cairo? The promise and reality of ICPD. Population Reference Bureau [Report]. Retrieved from https://www.prb.org/resources/what-was-cairo-the-promise-and-reality-of-icpd/.

Barbera, R. (2009). Community remembering: Fear and memory in a Chilean Shantytown. *Latin American Perspectives, 36*(5), 72–88.

Behnke, E. A. (2003). Embodiment work for the victims of violation: In solidarity with the community of the shaken. In C. Cheung, I. Chvatik, I. Copoeru, L. Embree, J. Iribarne, & H. R. Sepps (Eds.), *Essays in celebration of the founding of the organization of phenomenological organizations* (pp. 1–14). Prague, Czech Republic.

108 · References

Bernal, D. D., Burciaga, R., & Carmona, J. F. (2012). Chicana/Latina testimonies: Mapping the methodological, pedagogical, and political. *Equity & Excellence in Education, 45*(3), 363–372.

Bhattacharjee, A., & Silliman, J. (2002). *Policing the national body: Race, gender, and criminalization in the United States*. South End Press.

Biggs, M. A., Casas, L., Ramm, A., Baba, C. F., Correa, S. V., & Grossman, D. (2019). Future health providers' willingness to provide abortion services following decriminalization of abortion in Chile: A cross-sectional survey. *BMJ Open, 9*(10), 1–10. Retrieved from https://bmjopen.bmj.com/content/bmjopen/9/10/e030797.full.pdf.

Blofield, M. H., & Haaz, L. (2005). Defining democracy: Reforming the laws on women's rights in Chile, 1990–2002. *Latin American Politics & Society, 47*(3), 35–68.

Bruey, A. J. (2009). Neoliberalism and repression in poblaciones of Santiago de Chile. *Stockholm Review of Latin American Studies, 5*, 17–27.

Caputo, G. A. (2014). *Halfway house for women: Oppression and resistance*. Northeastern University Press.

Casas-Becerra, L. (1997). Women prosecuted and imprisoned for abortion in Chile. *Reproductive Health Matters, 5*(9), 29–36.

Casas, L. B. (2011). Women and reproduction: From control to autonomy? The case of Chile. *Journal of Gender, Social Policy & the Law, 12*(3), 427–519.

Casas, L., & Ahumada, C. (2009). Teenage sexuality and rights in Chile: From denial to punishment. *Reproductive Health Matters, 17*(34), 88–98.

Casas, L., & Herrera, T. (2012). Maternity protection vs. maternity rights for working women in Chile: A historic review. *Reproductive Health Matters, 20*(40), 139–147.

Casas, L., Vivaldi, L., Silva, M. C., Bravo, M. C., & Sandoval, C. N. F. (2013). La penalización del aborto como una violación a los derechos humanos de las mujeres. In Universidad Diego Portales Informe Annual Sobre Derechos Humanos en Chile 2013. Santiago, Chile: Universidad Diego Portales.

Casas, L., Vivaldi, L., Montero, A., Bozo, N., Alvarez, J. J., & Babul, J. (2022). Primary care and abortion legislation in Chile: A failed point of entry. *Developing World Bioethics, 23*(2), 154–165.

Center for Reproductive Law and Policy (1997). *Women of the world: Laws and policies affecting their reproductive lives: Latin America and the Caribbean*. Center for Reproductive Law and Policy.

Center for Reproductive Law and Policy (1998). *Women behind bars: Chile's abortion laws — A human rights analysis* (pp. 23–34). The Center for Reproductive Law and Policy and the Open Forum on Reproductive Health and Rights.

Center for Reproductive Rights (2010). *Dignity denied: Violations of the rights of HIV-positive women in Chilean health facilities*. Retrieved from http://reproductiverights.org/sites/crr.civicactions.net/files/documents/chilereport_single_FIN.pdf.

Center for Reproductive Rights (2015). *Chile: Reproductive rights at risk*. (Submission Brief 55th Session). Economic, Social and Cultural Rights Committee. Retrieved from http://www.reproductiverights.org/sites/crr.civicactions.net/files/documents/Submission_Brief_Chile_CESCR_55th_Session.pdf.

References • 109

Center for Reproductive Rights (2023). The world's abortion laws [Interactive Map]. Retrieved from https://reproductiverights.org/maps/worlds-abortion-laws/.

Cianelli, R., Ferrer, L., & McElmurry, B. J. (2008). HIV prevention and low-income Chilean women: Machismo, marianismo and HIV misconceptions. *Culture, Health & Sexuality, 10*(3), 297–306.

Collins, P., & Bilge, S. (2020). *Intersectionality*. Polity.

Crenshaw, K. (1991). Mapping the margins: Intersectionality, identity politics, and violence against women of color. *Stanford Law Review, 43*(6), 1241–1299.

Crenshaw, K. (2017). *On intersectionality: Essential writings*. The New Press.

Culliney, S. M., Peterson, M., & Royer, I. (2013). *The Mapuche struggle for land and recognition: A legal analysis*. Unrepresented Nations and Peoples Workshop. Lewis & Clark Law School, Portland, OR.

Cultural Survival (2019). Indigenous rights violations in Chile. *Prepared for the 100th Session of the Convention on the Elimination of Racial Discrimination*. Retrieved from https://www.culturalsurvival.org/sites/default/files/Chile_CERD_2019.pdf.

Dejarlais, R. (1997). *Shelter blues: Sanity and selfhood among the homeless*. University of Pennsylvania Press.

DeMello, M. (2014). *Body studies: An introduction*. Routledge.

Dolezal, L., & Petherbridge, D. (2017). *Body, self, other: The phenomenology of social Encounters*. State University of New York Press.

Eisenstein, Z. (2001). *Manmade breast cancers*. Cornell University Press.

Espinoza, O. (2008). Creating (in) equalities in access to higher education in the context of structural adjustment and post-adjustment policies: The case of Chile. *Higher Education, 55*, 269–284.

Estrada, D. (2007, December 8). *Rights-Chile: Workers massacre more relevant than ever 100 years on*. Inter Press Service News Agency. Retrieved from https://www.ipsnews.net/2007/12/rights-chile-workersrsquo-massacre-more-relevant-than-ever-100-years-on/#google_vignette.

Estrada, D. (2009a, October 29). *Rights-Chile: Stop violence against indigenous children—UNICEF*. Inter Press Service News Agency. Retrieved from http://www.ipsnews.net/2009/10/rights-chile-stop-violence-against-indigenous-children-unicef/.

Estrada, D. (2009b, November 2). *Chile: Teen pregnancy, a problem that won't go away*. Inter Press Service News Agency. Retrieved from http://www.ipsnews.net/2009/11/chile-teen-pregnancy-a-problem-that-wonrsquot-go-away/.

Farmer, P. (2005). *Pathologies of power: Health, human rights, and the new war on the poor*. University of California Press.

Faúndez, J. (1988). *Marxism and democracy in Chile: From 1932 to the fall of Allende*. Yale University Press.

Figueroa Huencho, V. (2021). Mapuche movements in Chile: From resistance to political recognition. *Georgetown Journal of International Affairs*, retrieved from https://gjia.georgetown.edu/2021/05/21/mapuche-movements-in-chile-from-resistance-to-political-recognition/.

Foucault, M. (1977). *Discipline & punishment: The birth of the prison*. Random House, Inc.

Foucault, M. (1990). *The history of sexuality, vol. 1: An introduction.* Vintage Books Edition.

Freire, P. (1985). *The politics of education: Culture, power, and liberation.* Bergin & Garvey.

Fried, G. (2006). Piecing memories together after state terror and policies of oblivion in Uruguay: The female political prisoner's testimonial project (1997–2004). *Social Identities, 12*(5), 543–562.

Galtung, J. (1969). Violence, peace, and peace research. *Journal of Peace Research, 6*(3), 167–191.

Galtung, J. (1990). Cultural violence. *Journal of Peace Research, 27*(3), 291–305.

Gurr, B. (2015). *Reproductive justice: The politics of health care for Native American women.* Rutgers University Press.

Hill Collins, P. (2019). *Intersectionality: As critical social theory.* Duke University Press.

Hill Collins, P., & Bilge, S. (2020). *Intersectionality: Key concepts.* Polity.

Hollander, J. A., & Einwohner, R. L. (2004). Conceptualizing resistance. *Sociological Forum, 19*(4), 533–554.

Htun, M. (2003). *Sex and the state: Abortion, divorce, and the family under Latin American dictatorships and democracies.* Cambridge University Press.

Jarroud, M. (2015, September 11). Antofagasta mining region reflects Chile's inequality. In *Global Issues: Social, Political, Economic, and Environmental Issues That Affect Us All.* Inter Press Service. Retrieved from https://www.globalissues.org/news/2015/09/11/21483.

Klein, N. (2007). *The shock doctrine: The rise of disaster capitalism.* Picador.

Kennedy, J. F. (1961, March 14). *Special message to the congress requesting appropriations for the Inter-American fund for social progress and reconstruction in Chile.* The American Presidency Project. Retrieved from https://www.presidency.ucsb.edu/documents/special-message-the-congress-requesting-appropriations-for-the-inter-american-fund-for.

Khan, A. (2014). Structural violence: A tale of three women from marginalized communities in Bangladesh. *International Journal of Minority and Group Rights, 21*, 547–556.

Kowalczyk, A. M. (2013). Indigenous peoples and modernity: Mapuche mobilization in Chile. *Latin American Perspectives, 40*(4), 121–135.

Larsson, N. (2020, June 5). Teargas is banned in warfare, it should not be used on the public. *Toward Freedom.* Retrieved from https://towardfreedom.org/story/teargas-is-banned-in-warfare-it-should-not-be-used-on-the-public/.

Luna, Z. (2020). *Reproductive rights as human rights: Women of color and the fight for reproductive justice.* New York University Press.

Maira, G., Casas, L., & Vivaldi, L. (2019). Abortion in Chile: The long road to legalization and its slow implementation. *Abortion Law Reform, 21*(2), 121–131.

Maira, G., Hurtado, J., & Santana, P. (2010). Feminist positions on abortion in Chile. *Women's Health Journal, 2*, 20–37.

Martinez, J. (2013). Family planning vs. women's rights: The case of quinacrine sterilization in Chile. *McNair Scholars Research Journal, 17*(9), 1–19.

Mazza, B. (2011). Women and the prison industrial complex: The criminalization of gender, race, and class in the war on drugs. *Dialogues Journal, 5*, 79–90.

McSherry, J. P., & Mejía, R. M. (2011). Chilean students challenge Pinochet's legacy. *NACLA Report on the Americas, 44*(6), 29–34.

Michaels, A. L. (1976). The Alliance for Progress and Chile's revolution in liberty, 1964–1970. *Journal of Interamerican Studies and World Affairs, 18*(1), 74–99.

Moenne, M. E. A. (2005). Embodying memory: Women and the legacy of the military government in Chile. *Feminist Review, 79*, 150–161.

Mohanty, C. T. (2003). *Feminism without borders: Decolonizing theory, practicing solidarity*. Duke University Press.

Mullen, M. (2015). Reassessing the focus of transnational justice: The need to move structural and cultural violence to the centre. *Cambridge Review of International Affairs, 28*(3), 462–479.

Mullings, B. (1999). Insider or outsider, both or neither: Some dilemmas of interviewing in a cross-cultural setting. *Geoforum, 30*, 337–350.

Muñoz Cabrera, P. (2010). *Intersecting violences: A review of feminist theories and debates on violence against women and poverty in Latin America*. London, UK: Central American Women's Network.

National Security Archive (2004). *Chile 1964: CIA covert support in Frei election detailed*. Retrieved from http://nsarchive.gwu.edu/news/20040925/.

Northrup, N., & Shifter, M. (2015, March). *Abortion and reproductive rights in Latin America: Implications for democracy* [Report]. Center for Reproductive Rights and Inter-American Dialogue. Retrieved from http://www.reproductiverights.org/sites/crr.civicactions.net/files/documents/IAD9794%20Repro%20Rights_web.pdf.

Núñez, N. R., & Torres, C. E. (2007). Mujeres migrantes Peruanas y salud reproductiva: Usarias de consultorios de salud de la zona norte de la region metropolitana. Fondo de Población de Naciones Unidas (UNFPA).

Parkins, W. (2000). Protesting like a girl: Embodiment, dissent and feminist agency. *Feminist Theory, 1*(1), 59–78.

Pernet, C. A. (2000). Chilean feminists, the international women's movement, and suffrage 1915–1050. *Pacific Historical Review, 69*(4), 663–688.

Pieper Mooney, J. E. (2007). Militant motherhood re-visited: Women's participation and political power in Argentina and Chile. *History Compass, 5*(3), 975–994.

Pieper Mooney, J. E. (2009). *The politics of motherhood: Maternity and women's rights in twentieth-century Chile*. University of Pittsburgh Press.

Pieper Mooney, J. E. (2015). *Family planning and reproductive rights in Chile*. Oxford Research Encyclopedia, Latin American History. Retrieved from http://latinamericanhistory.oxfordre.com/view/10.1093/acrefore/9780199366439.001.0001/acrefore-9780199366439-e-103.

Pieper Mooney, J. E., & Campbell, J. (2009). *Feminist activism and women's rights mobilization in the Chilean círculo de estudios de la mujer: Beyond maternalist mobilization*. Center for the Education of Women, University of Michigan. Retrieved from https://www.cew.umich.edu/wp-content/uploads/2021/05/Feminist-Activism-and-Women%E2%80%99s-Rights-Mobilization-in-the-Chilean-Ci%CC%81rculo-de-Estudios-de-la-Mujer-Beyond-Maternalist-MobilizationPieperMooney3-09_0.pdf.

112 • *References*

Poblamiento (2015). *Memoria Chilena, Biblioteca Nacional de Chile*. Retrieved from http://www.memoriachilena.cl/602/w3-article-93813.html.

Polk, B. B. (1972). Women's liberation: Movement for equality. In C. Safilios-Rothschild (Ed.) *Toward a sociology of women* (pp. 321–330). Xerox College Publishing.

Pollack, S. (2000). Reconceptualizing women's agency and empowerment: Challenges to self-esteem discourse and women's lawbreaking. *Women & Criminal Justice, 12*(1), 75–89.

Rayas, L. (1998). Criminalizing abortion: A crime against women. *NACLA Report on the Americas, 31*(4), 22–26.

Richards, P. (2004). *Pobladoras, Indígenas and the state: Conflicts over women's rights in Chile*. Rutgers University Press.

Richards, P. (2005). The politics of gender, human rights, and being Indigenous in Chile. *Gender & Society, 19*(2), 199–220.

Richards, P. (2010). Of Indians and terrorists: How the state and local elites construct the Mapuche in neoliberal multicultural Chile. *Journal of Latin American Studies, 42*(1), 59–90.

Roberts, D. (2016). *Killing the black body: Race, reproduction, and the meaning of liberty*. Penguin Random House.

Rojas, P. (2012). *La construccion del centro de Calama como region moral* (Unpublished doctoral dissertation). Universidad Católica del Norte, Facultad de Humanidades, Escuela de Psiocología, Antofogasta, Chile.

Ross, L., & Solinger, R. (2017). *Reproductive justice: An introduction*. University of California Press.

Salime, Z. (2014). New feminism as personal revolutions: Microrebellious bodies. *Signs, 40*(1), 14–20.

Saroj Bakhru, T. (2019). *Reproductive justice and sexual rights: Transnational perspectives*. Routledge.

Sepúlveda, E. (1996). *We, Chile: Personal testimonies of the Chilean arpilleristas*. Azul Editions.

Sepúlveda Swatson, D. (1998). De tomas de terreno a campamentos: Movimiento social y politico de los pobladores sin casa, durante las décadas de 60 y 70, en la periferia urbana de Santiago de Chile. *Boletin INVI, 35*, 103–115.

Shepard, B. (2000). The double discourse on sexual and reproductive rights in Latin America: The chasm between public policy and private actions. *Health and Human Rights, 4*(2), 111–143.

Shepard, B. (2006). *Running the obstacle course to sexual and reproductive health: Lessons from Latin America*. Praeger Publishers.

Shepard, B., & Casas Becerra, L. (2007). Abortion policies and practices in Chile: Ambiguities and dilemmas. *Reproductive Health Matters, 15*(30), 202–210.

Silliman, J. (2002). Introduction. In J. Silliman & A. Bhattacharjee (Eds.), *Policing the national body: Race, gender, and criminalization* (pp. ix–xxix). South End Press.

Silliman, J., Fried, M. G., Ross, L., & Gutiérrez, E. R. (2004). *Undivided rights: Women of color organize for reproductive justice*. South End Press.

Smith, A. (2005). *Conquest: Sexual violence and American Indian genocide.* Duke University Press.

Sturken, M. (1997). *Tangled memories: The Vietnam War, the AIDS epidemic, and the politics of remembering.* University of California Press.

Sultana, F. (2007). Reflexivity, positionality and participatory ethics: Negotiating fieldwork dilemmas in international research. *ACME: An International E-Journal for Critical Geographies, 6*(3), 374–385.

Sutton, B. (2010). *Bodies in crisis: Culture, violence, and women's resistance in neoliberal Argentina.* Rutgers University Press.

Sutton, B., & Vacarezza, N. L. (Eds.) (2021). *Abortion and democracy: Contentious body politics in Argentina, Chile, and Uruguay.* Routledge.

Tagle, J. E. (2006). *Discourses on women's suffrage in Chile 1865–1949.* [Master's thesis, Ponitificia Universidad Católica de Chile]. Retrieved from http://socialsciences.scielo.org/scielo.php?script=sci_arttext&pid=S0717-71942006000100002.

Tibbetts, A. (1994). Mamas fighting for freedom in Kenya. *Africa Today, 41*(4), 22–27.

Trumper, R. (1999). Healing the social body: Silence, terror, and (re)conciliation in neoliberal Chile. *Alternatives: Global, Local, Political, 24*(1), 1–37.

Vargas, G. A. M. (2008). Abortion in Chile: Contributions to the debate from women's perspective. *Women's Health Journal, 4,* 38–40.

Wade, A. (1997). Small acts of living: Everyday resistance to violence and other forms of oppression. *Contemporary Family Therapy, 19*(1), 23–39.

Waitzkin, H. (1983). Health policy and social change: A comparative history of Chile and Cuba. *Social Problems, 31*(2), 235–248.

Waitzkin, H. (2001). Social medicine then and now: Lessons from Latin America. *American Journal of Public Health, 91*(10), 1592–1601.

Waitzkin, H. (2005). Commentary: Salvador Allende and the birth of Latin American social medicine. *International Journal of Epidemiology, 34,* 739–741.

Walsh, D. M. (2011). *Women's rights in democratizing states: Just debate and gender justice in the public sphere.* Cambridge University Press.

Willen, S. S. (2007). Toward a critical phenomenology of illegality: State power, criminalization, and abjectivity among undocumented migrant workers in Tel Aviv, Israel. *International Migration, 45*(3), 8–38.

United Nations Special Rapporteur on the Right to Health (2011). *Interim report of the special rapporteur on the right of everyone to the enjoyment of the highest attainable standard of physical and mental health.* (Sixty-sixth session).

United Nations Women (1995, September). *The United Nations fourth world conference on women.* Platform for Action. Retrieved from http://www.un.org/women watch/daw/beijing/platform/health.htm.

Unrepresented Nations and Peoples Organization (2008, August 28). *Mapuche: Chile's hidden war.* Retrieved from https://old.unpo.org/article/8576.

Zibechi, R. (2009, November 13). *Toward reconstruction of the Mapuche nation.* MIRA: Feminism and Democracies. Retrieved from https://www.americas.org/6574/.

Index

1973 coup, 3, 19, 24, 29, 34, 69, 79–80, 96–97; US support for, 1–2, 14, 17. *See also* dictatorship

abortion complications, 3, 7, 11, 20–21, 23, 26, 30, 66, 69, 71
abortion law, 9, 11, 47, 74, 99; after return to democracy, 29; awareness of, 34; changes to, 2, 7; criminalizing abortion, ix, 3, 6–7, 13, 28, 95–96; effects of, 6–7; and typologies of violence, 98. *See also specific statutes*
abortion providers, 7–8, 34, 61, 62, 64, 71
abstinence, 9
activism, xi, 4–5, 23, 25, 29, 70, 80, 83, 87, 89, 106n2
Act on the Voluntary Termination of Pregnancy (VTP), 29
Adair, Vivyan C., 87
Afro-Colombians, 42
agency, 9, 13, 37, 43, 91, 97, 101–3; constraints on, 11–12, 23, 28, 35, 47, 49, 59–60, 67, 99; financial resources enabling, 61; and the politics of choice, 8, 57, 77, 100
Alejandra, 22, 28–29

allanamientos, 38, 81
Allende, Salvador, 2, 17, 23–24, 38, 39, 44, 80, 83; *La Realidad Médico-Social Chilena,* 20
Alma, 33, 43, 45, 47, 52–53, 55–57, 68
Americas, 2, 20. *See also individual countries*
Anaís, 4–5, 60–64, 67, 74–76, 91
Ani, 26, 30, 60, 62
anti-Communism, 19
anticonceptivos. See contraception
Anti-Terrorism Law (1984), 39–40
Antofogasta, Chile, 56
Araucanía Region, Chile, 16, 39, 51
Argentina, 15
Australia, ix
authoritarianism, 25, 81, 83–84. *See also* dictatorship; state terrorism
autonomy, x, 8, 29, 63, 99
Aylwin, Patricio, 40
Aymara people, 1

Bachelet, Michelle, 29, 86
Behnke, Elizabeth, 69
Bernal, Dolores Delgado, 93
Bill 1759 (2004), 47

116 · *Index*

birth control, 9, 22–23, 26, 47, 57, 68, 74. *See also* abstinence; condoms; contraception; morning after pill
black market abortions, 7–8, 72, 75, 77
Bolivia, 15, 33, 55–56
Burciaga, Rebeca, 93

Calama, Chile, 15, 33, 42–43, 52, 55–56, 68
Camila, 53–54
campamentos, 15, 22, 31–32, 55, 86
Campbell, Jean, 25, 84
cancer screenings, 30–31
capitalism, 1, 21, 43–44
carabiñeros, 66, 86–87
Carmona, Judith Flores, 93
Casas, Lidia, 24
Catholic Church, 3, 28–30, 33, 46–50, 56, 68, 75; opposition to divorce, 47
Catrileo, Matías, 41
Cementerio General, 2
Center for Reproductive Rights, 50
centering women, x, 6, 9, 12, 17, 59–78, 95–97, 100
Central America, x
Central Intelligence Agency (CIA), 1
Chemical Weapons Convention (1993), 87
Chicago Boys Chile Project, 25
Chilean Constitution, 5, 14, 39, 79
Chilean Independence, 39, 79
choice, 9, 27, 43, 46–48, 50, 54, 60–61, 70–71; and agency, 8, 57, 77, 100. *See also* pro-choice discourse
Civil Registry, 20
clandestine abortions, 7–9, 13, 22–23, 26–27, 61–77, 91, 93–94, 97–103
class, ix, 13, 15–16, 53, 79, 85–86, 88, 91, 94; and Catholicism, 46, 48; class equity, 4–5, 24; and colonialism, 38; and intersectionality, 12, 37, 41–42, 57, 78; middle-, 42–43, 61–62, 84; and migration, 3; shaping abortion, 5–8, 20, 26–28, 34, 60–62, 68, 96, 102–3; shaping reproductive health, 23–26, 44–46, 99; in social medicine, 24; upper-, 43, 45, 61, 84; working-, 20, 23, 68, 80, 87, 105n10. *See also* poverty
classism, 12, 44–45

Cold War, 19, 21, 24, 34
collectivity, 13, 41–42, 53–54, 73, 80, 86, 88–93, 102–3
Colombia, 15, 33, 42, 55
colonialism/imperialism, 9; settler colonialism, 10; Spanish, 3, 38, 46; US, 17. *See also* hacienda system
Communism, 4, 21, 39; anti-, 19
Communist Party, 14, 80
Communist Youth of Chile, 92
condoms, 4, 76
consciousness-raising, 82–83, 93
Constanza, 4–5, 40, 61, 63, 70–71
consultorios, 14, 20, 27, 30–32, 37–38, 42–43, 46–47, 52–55, 57, 97
contraception, 2, 22–28, 32, 46, 48–49; nonconsensual, 54–55. *See also* birth control; condoms; morning after pill
Convention on the Elimination of All Forms of Discrimination Against Women (CEDAW), 30
Copper-T IUD, 23, 27, 33, 54–55
coup d'état (1973), 3, 19, 24, 29, 34, 69, 79–80, 96–97; US support for, 1–2, 14, 17. *See also* dictatorship
critical phenomenology, 10, 13
cultural rights, 40
cultural violence, 11, 37, 51, 57, 77, 98–99
curettage, 55
Curinao, Carlos, 41

decriminalization, 3, 14, 19, 29–30, 33–34, 88–89
democracy, 19, 21, 40, 47, 84–85; abortion under, 28–34, 96, 100
dictatorship, 61, 68, 100; abortion under, 3, 5, 19, 24–30, 62, 96–97; US support for, 1–2, 14, 17; violence under, 1–2, 15, 38–39, 41, 81–83, 87, 98; women's movement under, 83–86. *See also* 1973 coup; authoritarianism; state terrorism
Dirección de Inteligencia Nacional (DINA), 26
direct violence, 11, 37, 51, 57, 98–100, 102
disappearance, 1–2, 14–15, 38, 81–82, 98
discrimination, 6, 17, 24, 30–31, 85; and cultural violence, 37–58; and institu-

tional violence, 54–57; shaping abortion, 7, 73–74; shaping reproductive health, 31, 33, 96–101

divorce, 47–48, 85

doctors, 20, 22, 30, 55, 61–62, 66, 68, 92

domestic violence, 4–5, 22, 46–48, 66, 84–85. *See also* intimate partner violence (IPV); violence against women

domestic workers, 4, 38, 40, 44–45, 99–100

double repression, 25

Ecuador, 15, 33, 55

Eisenstein, Zillah, 4

Elena, 81

Emilia, 19, 46, 54–55, 70

England, ix

Ercilla Region, Chile, 41

Esperanza, 55, 64, 69, 71, 90

Estrada, Daniela, 41, 79

family planning programs, 2, 8, 21, 23–24, 26, 28–29, 101

Farmer, Paul, 10, 12, 37

feminism, 1, 13, 15, 22–24, 28, 45, 83, 93; antiviolence activism, 48; classed, 41–42; middle-class, 42; reproductive rights activism, 29, 87–89, 91; socialist, 84

Fernanda, 32, 37–38

fetal disability, 8, 29, 34

forced sterilization, 9

foreign aid, 2, 21, 34

Fourth World Conference on Women (1995), 29

Francesca, 22, 24–25, 27, 81–82, 91

Francisco, 32, 42–43, 45, 50, 52, 68, 73, 101

Frei Montalva, Eduardo, 2, 21, 24, 26

Gabriella, 51

Gabriella Mistral Museum, 14

Galtung, Johan, 10–11, 27, 98

gender, 13, 15–16, 24–25, 80, 83, 88, 94; and Catholicism, 28; and cultural violence, 37–58; gender inequity, 6–8, 12, 38, 46–58, 82, 91, 96, 99, 102–3; gender norms, 3, 6, 8, 28, 34, 46, 50, 89; and intersectionality, 12, 86; shaping abortion,

5–9, 77–78, 99, 102–3; and structural violence, 34–35

gender-based violence, 6, 9. *See also* domestic violence; intimate partner violence (IPV); sexual violence; violence against women

gestational limitations, 8

Global North, ix, 9, 21

Global South, 7, 9

Gomperts, Rebecca, 3

Guevara, Che, 1, 88

guilt, 70, 74–77

hacienda system, 38, 46

Health Code (1931, Section 119), 28

herbal abortion, 60

Herrera, Tania, 24

human rights, x, 3, 9–19, 29–30, 34, 41, 79, 85, 87, 91, 99–100, 103

Hurtado, Josefina, 59, 91

I Choose Me, ix

illegality, 28, 30; shaping abortion, 4, 6–7, 12–13, 17, 20, 22, 26, 60–69, 72–77, 91–93, 98–99, 102–3

illegitimacy, 20, 105n2

illiteracy, 21, 40

immigrants, 3, 15, 39, 89, 99; marginalization of, 16, 33, 42–44, 55–57, 96, 98, 100. *See also* migration

incarceration, ix, 1, 3, 7, 9, 39, 82, 92

Incas, 79

incest, 8, 29, 51

Indigenous peoples, 1, 4, 86; and colonialism, 79; health care access for, 15; and land theft, 38; marginalization of, 16, 39–42, 54–55, 58, 96, 98. *See also individual nations and communities*

Indigenous Peoples Act (1993), 40

Indigenous rights, 39–42

individualism, 37, 42, 54

inequity, 83, 86–88, 94; and cultural violence, 37–58; gender inequity, 6–8, 12, 38, 46–58, 82, 91, 96, 99, 102–3; shaping abortion, x, 2, 5–17, 19–35, 59, 62, 77–78, 95–96, 98–103

infant mortality, 20, 33, 56

118 · *Index*

International Conference on Population and Development (ICPD, 1994), 29; Black Women's Caucus, 9
International Workers' Day, 86
intersectionality, 8, 12, 17, 22, 37, 41, 51, 57, 99, 100, 103
intimate partner violence (IPV), 4–5, 22, 46–48, 50–54, 66, 82, 84–85. *See also* domestic violence; violence against women
intrauterine devices (IUDs), 23, 55; non-consensual removal, 27–28. *See also* Copper-T IUD
Iquique, Chile, 79
Isadora, 23, 26–27, 29, 48, 83, 85
Isla Negra, Chile, 80
isolation, 7, 16–17, 27, 40–41, 50, 53, 57, 59–60, 70–73, 77, 93, 97, 100

Johanna, 33, 56

Katia, 87–89
Kennedy, John F.: *Alianza para el Progreso*, 21
Kenya, 88
Kikuyu women, 88

La Línea, 14
La Moneda, 14
land theft, 39–40
Latin America, 2, 14, 17, 21, 84, 93. *See also individual countries*
legalization, ix, 3, 29, 34
lesbians, 48, 76, 87, 89
liberation theology movement, 70
Londres 38, 14, 81
low-income women, 16, 23, 27
Luisa, 25, 30–31, 48, 51, 73
Lumen, Alex, 41

Macarena, 59, 62, 64–67, 69, 71–72, 75, 89, 92–93, 97, 101
machismo, 15, 37, 46–47, 52–53. *See also* patriarchy
Maira, Gloria, 59, 91
mandatory minimum sentencing, ix
mandatory reporting, 3, 26, 30, 33, 66
Mapuche people, 1, 4, 14, 16, 38–44, 51, 53–54, 70, 79, 86, 89–90
Mapundungun language, 39

Marcela, 52, 54, 62–63, 73, 75
March for the Disappeared, 1–2, 14
marginalization, 12, 16, 19, 25, 86, 89, 93–95; and cultural violence, 37, 39, 42, 44–45; shaping abortion, ix–x, 7, 9–10, 22, 27, 33–34, 61, 77–78, 96–101
Maria José, 31–32, 55
Maria Paz, 80
marianismo, 46
Marisol, 68
Marta, 45
Marxism, 39
maternal mortality, x, 2, 7, 11, 20–21, 23–24, 33
memory, 1–2, 14, 81
Mercedes, 25, 80–83
methodology of book, 13–17
Mexico, 62
migration, 47, 55–56; to cities, 20, 38; forced, 9. *See also* immigrants
militarization, 41
military rule, 2–3, 28, 34, 39
mining, 15, 33, 43, 52, 55, 79
Ministry of Health, 30
miscarriage, 55, 71
misoprostol, 55, 62–66, 71–72, 75, 89, 92, 106n1
Mohanty, Chandra Talpade, 95, 97
moral zones, 43
morning after pill, 29, 48–49
motherhood, 28, 82, 101; state meanings of, 21; as womanhood, 46–47, 50
Mullings, Beverley, 16
Muñoz Cabrera, Patricia, 51, 57
Museum of Memory and Human Rights, 14
mutual aid, 91

National Prosecutor of Chile, 50
neighborhood health centers (NHC), 20, 105n11. See also *consultorios*
neoliberalism, 19, 30, 34, 38–39, 44. *See also* privatization
Neruda, Pablo, 80
Netherlands, 3
nongovernmental organizations (NGOs), 13, 22–23, 28, 44, 49, 54, 83
nudity, 87–88, 102
Nuñez, Nuria, 56

Index • 119

oppression, 6, 9, 35, 84, 87–89, 93–94, 100; internalized, 7, 74–77, 97, 102; intersectional, 10, 12, 37, 42–43, 57, 78; intersex, 98
overpopulation discourse, 19, 21, 24

Pablo, 44
Pacificación de la Araucanía, 39
Paloma, 44–45, 47, 53, 60, 65–68, 99, 101
Paola, 24–25, 44, 47, 50, 81, 83–86
Pap test, 30–31, 55
parental authorization, 8
paternalism, 37–38, 55, 102
patriarchy, 1, 8–9, 12, 82; and women's roles, 25. See also *machismo*
patrones, 38, 40, 101
Paz, 4–5, 50, 62–65, 71–73, 75–76, 89, 92–93
pedophilia, 29, 53. *See also* sexual violence
Peru, 15, 33, 44, 47, 53, 55–56, 99
Pía, 23, 28, 59, 61–62, 69, 91–92, 97
Pieper Mooney, Jadwiga E., 22–23, 25, 84
Pilar, 63, 66–68, 71, 73, 82
Pinochet, Augusto, 5, 44–45; abortion policy, 2–3, 28–29, 30, 39; discrimination under, 14–15, 38; Indigenous policy, 39; Política de Populación, 24; population policy, 2–3, 19, 24–28, 30, 39; US support for, 17; violence under, 1–2, 38, 81–82, 92, 98. *See also* 1973 coup; dictatorship
Pinochet, Lucía Hiriart, 25
Plaza Brasil, 86
poblaciónes, 14, 22–25, 27, 30–31, 54, 63–65, 67–68, 70, 82, 86; and *consultorios*, 20; definition, 15–16, 105n10; targeted for *allanamientos*, 38; and *tomas de terrenos*, 80–81; women's leadership in, 85
police violence, 9, 40–41, 80–81, 86–87. *See also* state violence
popular education, 14, 82–83, 89
popular family, 83
population control, 2, 21, 29, 34, 37
poverty, 2, 4, 11, 15–16, 25, 80, 89, 105n10; cycle of, 45; and education, 45; and Indigeneity, 40, 42; and overpopulation discourse, 21, 24; in *poblaciónes*, 105n10; and reproductive health care, 33–34, 38; shaping abortion, 6, 8–9, 22, 58; and

social medicine, 20; and structural violence, 52, 56–57
privatization, 2, 25–26, 39, 45. *See also* neoliberalism
pro-birth policies, 24
pro-choice discourse, 8–9
pro-life discourse, 8–9
pronatalism, 2, 28
public health, 15, 21–22, 31, 33–34, 42, 54–55, 57, 71, 87, 100; under Allende, 2, 20, 23; under Pinochet, 2–3, 26–28, 30; and social medicine, 20. See also *consultorios*; neighborhood health centers (NHC); social medicine

Quechua people, 15
queerness, 9, 48

race, ix, 16, 57, 80, 86, 94; and colonialism, 46; and cultural violence, 37–44; and indigeneity, 39–44; and intersectionality, 12, 78; racial equity, 4; shaping abortion, 5–9, 34, 96, 99, 102–3
racialization, ix
racism, 4, 12, 15, 33, 40, 42, 44, 56–57, 100; anti-Indigenous, 40; internalized, 15
Rafael, 60
Rayen, 40–42, 53–55, 86, 90
reproductive justice, x, 9
reproductive rights, x, 7, 9, 19, 24, 28–30, 49, 62, 96
reproductive sovereignty, 9
resistance, 1–2, 13, 17, 31, 79; Mapuche, 41; and marginality, 101–3; women's, 78–94, 97–98
Richards, Patricia, 39, 86
Rocío, 23, 28
Roe v. Wade, ix
Rojas, Pablo, 43
Rounds, Mike, ix

Salime, Zakia, 88
Santana, Paula, 59, 91
Santiago, Chile, 1, 14–15, 23, 25, 31, 53–54, 70, 80, 86
Sepúlveda, Emma, 25
Servicio Nacional de la Mujer (SERNAM), 52, 85–86
sexism, 44, 57, 105n2

120 · Index

sexual education, 2, 23, 26, 48, 57
sexual violence, 3, 8, 9, 29, 34, 38, 47, 50, 52–54, 64; state-sponsored, 39, 51. *See also* pedophilia; violence against women
sex work, 33, 42–44, 56, 76, 89
shame, 7, 42, 60, 67, 74–77, 88, 90
Shepard, Bonnie, 43
silence, 8, 39, 60, 67–70, 77, 81, 93, 97–98, 102
single mothers, 4, 15, 20, 82
Sister Maria, 33, 56
slow violence, 10
social control, 23, 34
socialism, 21, 44, 83–84
social justice, 9, 59, 84, 95, 103
social medicine, 19–21, 34, 79
solidarity, 17, 80, 83, 86–98, 102–3
sonda technique, 22–23, 62–63, 66, 68
South Dakota, ix
Spanish colonialism, 3, 38–39, 46, 79
spousal authorization, 8; for contraception, 47
state terrorism, 25, 81. *See also* authoritarianism; dictatorship
state violence, x, 1, 2, 9, 38, 70, 79, 86–87, 97; against Indigenous peoples, 39–41. *See also* police violence
statutory rape law, 32–33
stillbirths, 56
structural violence, 10–11, 19, 27, 34–35, 37, 57, 59
student movement, 5, 14, 88, 105n3
Sultana, Farhana, 17
Sutton, Barbara, 12, 17, 73, 79, 89, 94

Tamara, 49–50
teen pregnancy, 26, 57

Temuco, Chile, 16, 40–41
Temucuicui, Chile, 41
therapeutic abortion, 3, 28
tomas de terrenos, 5, 16, 31, 80, 82, 88, 105n3
Torres, Carmen, 56
torture, 1, 14–15, 38–39, 79, 81–82, 98
Trumper, Ricardo, 38, 42

undocumented people, 33, 55–57
"unfit mother" discourse, 23
unions, 44, 86, 93
United Nations Children's Emergency Fund (UNICEF), 41
United Nations Special Rapporteur on the Right to Health, 1, 9, 95, 99
United States, ix–x, 3, 16, 34, 41; backing 1973 coup, 1–2, 14, 17; role in Chile, 17, 20–21. *See also individual states*
University of Chile, 23, 88
US Supreme Court, ix

Valparaiso, Chile, 15–16
Vietnam, 21
Viña del Mar, Chile, 15–16, 31, 37
violence against women, 37, 50–51, 53, 70, 89, 99. *See also* domestic violence; gender-based violence; sexual violence
violence typology, 10–12, 98–99
vulnerability, 7, 12, 43, 57, 62, 64, 72–73, 77, 98, 99

Waitzkin, Howard, 20
War on Drugs, ix
Women on Waves, 3
women's rights, 9, 13, 17, 19, 24, 28–30, 47, 51, 77, 79–80, 82–89, 96, 99
workers' rights, 14, 86–87

MICHELE EGGERS-BARISON is an associate professor in the School of Social Work at California State University, Chico.

The University of Illinois Press
is a founding member of the
Association of University Presses.

Composed in 10.25/13 Marat Pro
with Trade Gothic LT Std display
by Lisa Connery
at the University of Illinois Press

University of Illinois Press
1325 South Oak Street
Champaign, IL 61820-6903
www.press.uillinois.edu